Fifty years of London store publicity and display

SHOWING OFF

Ruth Artmonsky

For Stella, Becky and Sally, whose very existence keeps me going.

Published by Artmonsky Arts
Flat 1, 27 Henrietta Street
London WC2E 8NA
www.ruthartmonsky.com
ruthartmonsky@yahoo.co.uk
Tel. 020 7240 8774

Text © Ruth Artmonsky 2013

Designed by David Preston Studio
www.davidprestonstudio.com

Printed in England by Northend Creative Print Solutions
Clyde Road, Heeley, Sheffield, S8 0TZ

ISBN 978-0-9573875-1-5

Previous spread
Harrods, pen drawing, David Gentleman.

CONTENTS

INTRODUCTION

This book came about because of one woman, Natasha Kroll of Simpson's of Piccadilly. I had a lingering guilt at excluding her from a previous book – *Designing Women*; I had argued with my strong-willed and more knowledgeable book designer that *Designing Women* was primarily about women who had worked in, or for, advertising agencies and Natasha was marginal to this delineation.

Yet I had read, and heard gossip, that Natasha was a 'character' so, added to my guilt at turning her down, was a reluctance to lose a good story. However, what started out to be a modestly conceived biography of one display person quickly morphed, with the help of Google, archivists, and a few well-informed friends, into this tome, peopled with a myriad of 'personalities' against a London retail backcloth.

Although it is impossible with a title like 'Showing Off' to totally ignore the well-trodden route of the Edwardian grandeur of London stores, I have tried to focus more on the many, now largely forgotten, personalities of publicity and display, and what it was like to be part of the London store scene for the first part of the 20th century.

Opposite
A Lucking window display, Liberty's, early 1950s.

SHOWING OFF THE BUILDINGS

'…a store in every aspect, is an extension of the advertising idea, an idea that should permeate the whole building; façade; window; signs; and even down to the garments of the commissionaire and sales people. It should be the union of the architectural and merchandising.'

Joseph Emberton, *Art & Industry*, 1936

Up to the late 18th century there was little to 'show off' about shopping in London; shops as we know them now hardly existed, let alone stores. What are now the main shopping streets were spawned from ancient highways, some still rough tracks. Oxford Street was part of a former Roman road from East Anglia to the south coast; the King's Road, a private route for the monarch to Hampton Court; Piccadilly described as no more than a muddy lane; the Brompton Road a mere lane leading to the village of Brompton; and Kensington High Street, a narrow shabby thoroughfare, part of a coaching road to the West Country.

Such shops as did exist were little more 'show' worthy than the roads, some still merely the houses of craftsmen making goods for sale. A few of our modern stores, as Selfridges, Austin Reed's and Simpson's were built from scratch, but most London stores originated from small shops, mainly drapers or haberdashers, acquired with some optimism by young would-be entrepreneurs. Heal's started as a workshop selling beds and bedding, moving to Tottenham

Previous page
Construction of Harrods, 1901 building.

10

Heal's, 1854, architect J. Morant Lockyer.

Court Road in 1818; in 1812 George Swan and William Edgar took over a haberdasher's shop on the north side of Piccadilly; Thomas Dickens had a draper's shop in Oxford Street in the 1790s; Harvey Nichols was a linen shop on the corner of Knightsbridge and Sloane Street in 1834, and so on. Harrods and Fortnum & Mason were exceptions in that their origins lay with food rather than fabrics.

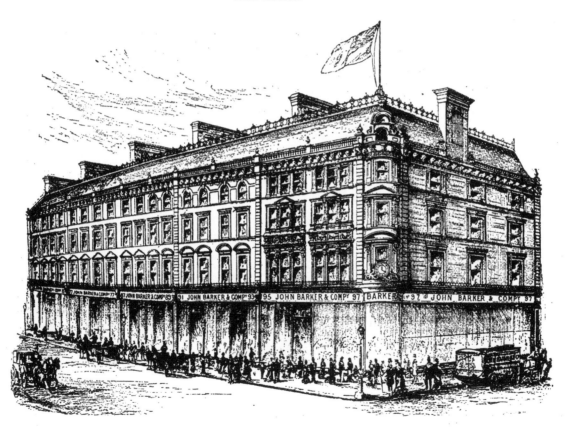

Harvey Nichols' new building, 1900.

The transformation of most of these small shops into stores followed much the same route – the shops would tend to start with workshops attached and living quarters above. Then the workshops would be hived off, and the owners, if successful, would move their families out to the burgeoning affluent suburbs; Harrods still had flats above the store until well into the 20th century. Then came acquisitions – on either side, down the street, and behind the shop; sometimes this was random, when a property came up for sale, which often meant that customers would have to go out on to the street to re-enter through another door if they wanted a different department. There were occasions when stores, such as Barkers, Harrods and Liberty's, grew over and around small retailers who resisted buy-outs.

Derry & Toms building, 1908.

In the case of both Regent Street and Kensington High Street, the actual building of 'show off' roads facilitated the growth of warehouses and emporia into full-blown stores. The concept of a grand avenue sweeping down from Regent's Park towards the Houses of Parliament was already being muted late in the 18th century, and in 1813 the New Street Act was passed, enabling the Crown to purchase the land for the venture. The story of John Nash's contribution to the development of Regent Street is familiar ground – accounts of his questionable roles, with conflict of interest, as architect, planner, overseer, developer and estate agent. Regent Street is claimed to be the first London road to have been designed specifically for shopping with:

> … shops appropriated to articles of taste and fashion will … arrange themselves … and the stream of fashion be directed to a new Street … where there will be room for all the fashionable shops to be assembled … with colonnades to protect shoppers and divide shops from lodgings above.

And arrange themselves they did, from Swan & Edgar which gobbled up the Piccadilly end, to Peter Robinson that spread itself at Oxford Circus. Kensington High Street is another example of how road and store development went hand in hand. In the 1860s the Metropolitan Board of Works had widened what had been a rather down-at-heel narrow road and had built on it a row of shops. In 1870 John Barker took the lease on two of these, numbers 91 and 93. Within three years he had bought up adjoining properties on the High Street and to the rear in Ball Street. Throughout the 1880s, he added to his portfolio, so that by 1890 he owned some twenty-eight shops, east along the High Street towards Young Street, and west to King Street. Meanwhile Joseph Toms and Charles Derry were building up their own little empire of some twelve shops from numbers 99 to 119, and the brothers Ponting were similarly occupied. Eventually Barker bought up both Pontings and Derry & Toms – Kensington High Street had been transformed into a shopping Mecca.

14

The new roads helped to 'show off' their buildings, and the store buildings themselves competed as to which was the largest, the grandest, and, at times, the most grandiose. Stores such as Whiteley's had started the trend early in Victoria's reign, but it was the store building and rebuilding from the end of the century up to WWI that provided the great 'show offs', both for their façades and their interiors. Although, perhaps, architecturally and technically, they were behind their continental equivalents, such as Samaritaine and Galeries Lafayette in Paris and Messel's Wertheim store in Berlin, they set out to compete in size if not in grandeur.

Harrods was built, and rebuilt, with its various acquisitions during the 1880s and 1890s. With Richard Burbidge at the helm, and C.W. Stephens as architect, the grand Brompton Road façade, and its building extending behind to Hans

PICCADILLY CIRCUS, LONDON.

Piccadilly Circus with Swan & Edgar c.1920s.

D.H. Evans building, built 1893.

SELFRIDGE & Co., Ltd., OXFORD STREET, LONDON, W.

(Midway between Bond Street and Marble Arch)

Road, was completed in 1905. Trading continued throughout the rebuild. Tim Dale in his history of Harrods described the result as:

> … comprehensively, the exuberant spirit of the Edwardian age. Everything – its great dome, its embellished pediment with Britannia receiving the produce of the world, its rich detailing, its pillars and urns and ballustrades – seems to encapsulate this high summer of the British Empire.

Selfridges, planned and built from scratch, by an American entrepreneur and an American architect, epitomised turn of the century store 'showing off'. The building, at the start, was some 249 feet long and 150 feet deep, had eight floor levels and five staircases with nine lifts. But it was the store's façade that made the greatest impact, with its iconic columns stretching over three floors.

17

Army & Navy Store, entrance, 1920s.

Austin Reed's foyer, with Joseph Pemberton's lift doors.

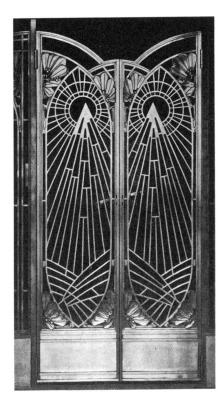

Close-up of Pemberton's lift doors for
Austin Reed, 1926.

In a 1940 tribute to Gordon Selfridge, Lord Ashfield, Chairman of London Transport said:

> I would like to pay a tribute to the magnificent enterprise, high endeavour and hard work which led to the transformation of Oxford Street by Mr. Selfridge ... So successful was Mr. Selfridge in attracting the public to his store, that at one time I almost thought we should have renamed Bond Street station, Selfridges ...

With WWI behind them, many London stores set about rebuilding programmes, including the Army & Navy, Fortnum & Mason's and Waring & Gillow. And it was in the post-WWI period that stretches of Regent Street were rebuilt, overseen by Sir Reginald Blomfield in order to ensure reasonable conformity in the rebuild plans of the separate establishments. This was achieved largely by the use of Portland stone for the façades, as with Austin Reed's and Swan & Edgar's. Liberty's complied reluctantly as far as its Regent Street frontage was concerned but went for a Tudor fantasia along Marlborough Street. Austin Reed had toured America with his architect Percy Westwood, when he also decided to redevelop his Regent Street site. Inspired by the American visit, Westwood, in advance of many other store architects, used steel framing and thus was able to open up the sales floors; but the overall result was a curious mixture of early art deco and, as with Liberty's, some Tudor revival. The modernist elements included Joseph Emberton's strikingly designed balconies and lift.

Liberty's, which presented a conventional front along Regent Street, totally succumbed to the neo-Tudor craze with its second building – Ivor Stewart-Liberty and a fellow director John Llewellyn were both under the spell of the Tudors [Llewellyn although living in a neo-Tudor house had genuine Tudor woodwork in it]. They retained as their architects father and son, Edwin and Stanley Hall, who appear to have been totally sympathetic to such tastes. Besides the oak and teak timbers for the staircase and panelling,

Liberty's 'tudor' interior, E.T. & E.S. Hall, 1924.

the back building was festooned with Tudor coats-of-arms, shields of Tudor personalities and much more of the same ilk. Although this may have been a great 'show off' for potential customers the architectural press was completely bemused by it all and fell back on such comments as 'quaint' and 'well-crafted'.

By the 1930s art deco was in full swing when it came to London store frontages for their redevelopments, as with Derry & Tom's and Barker's; for extensions, as with Heal's; and with new-builds as Simpson's of Piccadilly and Peter Jones. It took some three and a half years to rebuild Derry & Toms, which opened in 1933. Its architect was Bernard George, who was later to become a director of the store and to work on the Barker's new wonderfully towered store. Derry & Toms remained open during the rebuild except for the last few days when their advertisements fanfared:

> An army of experts comes in … artists to do amazing things with modern lights … people to lay miles and miles of deep-pile carpets … workers with wood and glass and metal … when the work is done we shall say to you 'Come back again – to this beautiful and most modern store.'

Derry & Toms most 'showing off' feature of their rebuild, not finished until 1938, was its roof garden, which was described as the kind 'a child would demand of its fairy godmother'. It included a Spanish garden [wrought iron, Moroccan pergola, fountains, coloured tiles]; a 16th century English garden [lavender, heliotrope, oak benches and urns]; and an English water garden [green lawn, flowing stream with carp, waterfall with willows].

Simpson's building was one showing the fullest expression of 'modernism' at the time. Its architect, Joseph Emberton, had split with Westwood after the completion of Austin Reed's, and had become one of the leading 'modernists'. The store opened in 1936, and was marked by its novel steel framing [modified by LCC regulations], its strong horizontal bands of windows, its wide open floor space, its immense light fitting filling the stair well, and its smooth art deco fittings and interior design to which Moholy-Nagy brought the simplified

D.H. Evans' new building, 1937.

Simpson's, façade at night, built 1936.

Simpson's, stairwell, 1936.

Peter Jones under construction, opened 1936.

Bauhaus tradition. As with Selfridges, Derry & Toms, and most other London stores when they were being launched, or relaunched, the press was kept up-to-date on what was about to astonish Piccadilly shoppers:

> ... there will rise during the next year a great new, and modern, men's store ... Certainly no store devoted exclusively to men's wear has ever occupied so commanding and exceptional position ...

Peter Jones was to have a similar dominating affect in Sloane Square as Simpson's had in Piccadilly. The building clearly shows the influence of continental architects of the time, as Eric Mendelsohn, whose designs were

Barbara Hepworth watching the placement of her sculpture on the John Lewis building, 1963.

characterized by strong geometric lines and long strips of horizontal windows. William Crabtree, the architect of Peter Jones, had worked in Pemberton's office before being retained by the John Lewis Partnership. In addition, for Peter Jones, the Partnership had C.H. Reilly as a consultant and Slater & Moberly as contract supervisors. The building, started in 1932, was completed in 1936. Its sweeping curtain wall of glass, curving along the King's Road, appears unsupported, its uprights being so slender. The 'show off' staircase, characteristic of so many other London stores, swung its way down to the basement.

The next round of store rebuilding was necessary as a result of bombing raids in WWII. Few London stores survived totally intact, but the Oxford Street ones were most badly hit. Bourne & Hollingsworth, one of the fin-de-siecle buildings, later remodelled in the art deco style, was holed in part of its interior, but was able to carry on business. Peter Robinson, in Oxford Circus, was similarly affected, whilst Selfridges, amongst other damage, lost its roof garden, never to be reopened. But it was John Lewis which suffered most, and although it carried on business during rebuilding, a new building was not finally completed until 1960, Barbara Hepworth's iconic 'Winged Figure' being attached in 1962.

As the development of London's thoroughfares enabled stores to grow and 'show off', so, in time, did the splendours of the store buildings endow character to their streets, so that going to Regent Street, Oxford Street, Knightsbridge or Kensington High Street inevitably meant 'going shopping'.

John Lewis' original building of 1864, image 1885.

John Lewis rebuilt, 1964.

SHOWING OFF
THE WINDOWS

In an article in the journal *The Imprint* in 1913, one W.B. Dingley, writing on the shop window of the time, bemoaned:

> There still appear to be many tradesmen who cannot be made to see the value and importance of the shop window; who just go on using it as a store cupboard, a place in which to deposit a load of goods when not wanted at the moment.

The London stores were no exemption to this. Images of Swan & Edgar's windows in 1906 showed every inch of one window space crammed with hats, and its neighbour crammed with lace accessories – no background visible in either; and a picture of John Barker's grocery window, at much the same time, contained literally hundreds of tins, stacked to the ceiling with only the trade cards breaking up the monotony of it all. Harrods was perhaps something of an exception, for although its goods displayed in its food halls tended to excess – bird upon bird, cheese upon cheese – so that one 'couldn't see for looking', it had started by the 1910s to actually 'dress', or as it was called at the time 'trim', its windows. Books on the subject of window display, began to be published and started to use such words as 'harmony', 'repetition' and 'symmetry', and to urge 'trimmers' to show their goods to best advantage and encourage them to think 'colour'.

> Chreveul, the eminent French chemist, whose work on colour stands pre-eminent, gives it as his opinion that the white edging and facing on a soldier's uniform brightens it in proportion of one to ten. This being so, then, judiciously, introduce such shades as will make the window bright and attractive.

The major skill seemingly required of display personnel, at least for those working in stores selling materials and fashion, and these would have been the majority of pre-WWI stores, was 'draping':

An early Jaeger crammed window.

Gems washable stands, 1920.

To simply place a piece of material over a dummy and allow it to drape itself is now quite out of date ... Much care and practice must be exercised before a high degree of skill is acquired and only perseverance will enable the beginner to overcome the early and most difficult stages of this art.

Folding, pleating, plaiting, hanging, waterfalling, wheatsheafing – the combinations seem endless, and obsessive:

A golden rule which should always be borne in mind is to never be guilty of overcrowding but to give every fold an opportunity of exhibiting itself to the best advantage.

But then Gordon Selfridge arrived and window display was never to be the same again. Gordon Honeycombe wrote of the display scene before Selfridges impact:

Until the advent of Gordon Selfridge, store windows in London were merely used as selling places in which quantities of goods, with their prices marked, were put on show. There was little idea of design, colour matching, composition, or themes, and hardly a window was lit at night, when blinds or curtains would be lowered or shutters drawn.

Selfridge was a showman at heart, and his often extravagant 'showing off' was only tempered by the intelligence and aesthetic sensitivity of his first displayman, Edward Goldsman. Stores had practiced the odd 'stunt' in their windows before Selfridge, as when Swan & Edgar in 1904 had a live model on show and offered £10 if anyone could make him smile; but no-one had the chutzpah of Selfridge, unrestrained by British display tradition. Windows began to tell a story, to be linked to topical events, and, an innovation, to be linked to the decoration of the whole building. Most frequently cited are the Selfridges windows for the Coronation of George v and Queen Mary in June 1911 'showing off' the history of British Royalty – royal emblems were mounted on a crimson valance along the outside of the store with twelve foot high shields bearing historical arms – flags abounded, everything was lit up – it was the talk of the town. Selfridge is said to have claimed that his store was the third biggest attraction for sightseers in London after Buckingham Palace and the Tower of London!

After WWI London store display people found themselves with large open window spaces to arrange rather than cram. Except for the competing giants

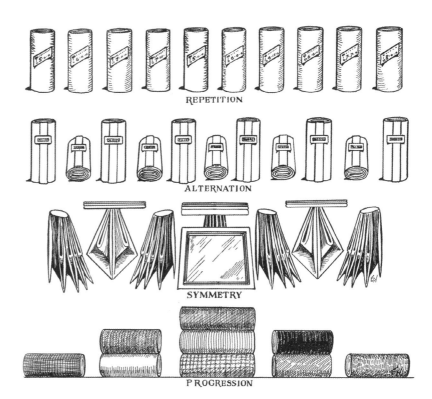

Suggested ways of displaying material, c.1910s.

– Selfridges and Harrods – this proved something of a challenge to their ingenuity. One pundit suggested they 'spread the goods from end to end'. Unsure as to how to use space, dressers began to surround, if not swamp, their merchandise with foliage – branches, bunches, vases and urns full. Well into the 1920s, whatever merchandise was being displayed, foliage, from single flowers to whole trees, would be placed to set it off, as if people would be embarrassed by seeing the merchandise unadorned, naked. John Barkers would always have a vase of flowers accompanying their fur coats; the Army & Navy found it essential to enclose their confectionery in wreaths; even Selfridges had

Furniture sale, Derry & Toms, 1925.

Vine-laden pergola display of men's shirts, Selfridges, 1925.

their male mannequins sitting amidst branches. All of this was encouraged by such firms of shop fitters as Zwart, who regularly advertised the availability of artificial beech, maple, vines, grapes, even lupins, assuring the stores that 'every care is taken to ensure that the natural form is copied in the minutest detail', and urging window dressers to 'drape their show cards with foliage' for their Autumn displays.

Show cards and price tickets were another obsession of the 1920s displays, 'placed alongside the merchandise, attached to the goods, suspended over them' to key up the chief selling points and to get the customer at least to pause a moment and give some thought to what they were seeing. Every issue of *Display*, throughout the '20s, contained articles on show cards, with such advisory platitudes as 'if you can't be original aim for neatness and dignity' or

Whiteley's display of sponges with display cards, 1920s.

be as imaginative as you can but not 'grotesque, overdone or startling'. Whole pages of the journal were devoted to suggested phrases for the cards to bear, particularly when it came to sales time:

> As we have so often urged, it is short-sighted policy to put 'startingly low priced articles' where there are only one or two of these articles. This results in a wild scramble from an undesirable class of customer …

Foliage and show cards, in hindsight, look pretty trivial when one remembers that on the Continent, Paris was mounting its influential Exposition des Arts

Decoratif in 1925, and Gropius was developing his Bauhaus ideas in Weimar from 1919. With a few exceptions London stores were still 'arranging' their windows whilst Continental and American stores were 'designing' theirs. There seems to have generally been a feeling of inferiority and impotency in London exemplified by such words of self-abasement as those of Harry Trethowan of Heals declaiming that London windows were just not good

Evening gown display, Peter Robinson, 1921.

enough. Even *Commercial Art*, whose aim was to promote good design, ran a series of articles over several months extolling German department stores as models for London to imitate. One such article compared the proactive approach of German displays with the passivity of British ones, showing the Germans deriving ideas from contemporary art and integrating their displays more effectively with store advertising. And both *Commercial Art* and *Display* lauded German display education over anything that was going on in England, quoting both state schools and, more frequently, the Reimann School in Berlin, the most progressive of its kind offering courses in window display.

Even when it came to aspects such as lighting, that London stores were beginning to experiment with, the Germans were said to have got there first:

Early use of photography displaying best-selling book, Selfridges, 1931.

> The new Liberty windows in Regent Street, London, have revealed a system
> of lighting new to this country. It has, however, been used for many years by
> leading Berlin and Vienese stores.

Liberty's 'new system' consisted of installing in the ceiling of each window opaque glass above which were placed light units. The light reflected down and this made it diffused over the merchandise. The likes of Osram and Magda opened offices near Oxford Street and began advertising campaigns directed at the stores. By 1925 *Display* was claiming:

> Display men are definitely converted to the use of good lighting as a means
> of enhancing the value of a display and are as qualified to deal with the
> subject as engineers.

A few London stores were just beginning to glance towards continental modernism for their windows in the 1920s, perhaps stirred by the arrival of Galleries Lafayette in Regent Street in 1927, [taking over the premises of Swears & Wells], and of Serge Chermayeff arriving at Waring & Gillows in 1928. Austin Reed's appointed its progressive displayman, R.W. Shorter, and many of the stores were now not merely arranging their windows, but trying to tell some sort of story in them, to catch the passer-by. This was helped by the arrival of the 'headed' mannequin, making scenes more realistic. Yet many stores in the 1920s still had the old stuffed torsos alongside the new models, often in the same window. Display suppliers competed with each other as to which could supply the most lifelike mannequins, most made of wax or sometimes coated with papier-mâché. Most of these came from Paris, with Parnell's carrying 'wax mannequins of distinguished beauty' by Louis Tussaud; whilst Sage imported Pierre Imans models, and were to continue to do so for the next decade or so.

Austin Reed's, in spite of the 'period' rooms in its new store in 1926, was a precursor of the modernism that was to flower in London stores in the 1930s.

Display of Pierre Imans wax mannequins, 1925.

A rarity, a woman display consultant and supplier, 1935.

THE "PIERRE IMANS" MANNEQUIN

EXHIBIT AT OUR SHOWROOMS :

58-62 GRAY'S INN ROAD, W.C.

THE MOST ADVANCED TYPES OF WAX ART CAN BE SEEN
AND PURCHASED FOR IMMEDIATE DELIVERY

FREDK. SAGE & CO., LIMITED

58-62, GRAY'S INN ROAD, LONDON, W.C.1

13b, Margaret Street, - W.1   92, Wood Street, - E.C.2.
8, Portland Street, Manchester   35, St. Mary Street, Cardiff

TOM TITT designs for display exclusively for PEARCE & CO

"Shirts which provoke admiration"!

Consult Katharine Pearce
for distinguished display.

PEARCE & CO ST. GEORGE'S STUDIO
HARLEY MEWS SOUTH,
WIGMORE STREET. W.I.
TELEPHONE: LANGHAM 2792.

Its advertising manager, Donald McCullough, commissioned artists of note, as Tom Purvis and McKnight Kauffer, to produce promotional material and they, along with Shorter, launched the image of the 'modern man' that the flaneur strolling along Regent Street would see displayed in Austin Reed's windows. Shorter was one of the first to use photography in display, specifically for Reed's own collar range 'Summit'. By the end of the '20s, Shorter was being described as the most 'followed' displaymanin the country, and Austin Reed's windows as:

> … the finest of their kind in the world … whatever decorations, fittings or settings are in Austin Reed's windows, these accessories do not fight for preeminence above the goods. It is the merchandise so cleverly treated, both individually and as a whole, that stands out conspicuously and attractively.

Shorter was fully supported in his designs by Austin Reed who wrote:

> If every retailer realized how loudly his windows proclaim his business he would see to it that he had an experienced specialist to broadcast through these loud-speakers.

Yet such examples must have been the exception, for in 1929 and 1930 *Commercial Art* was still deploring the backwardness of most London store windows in comparison with their Continental and American rivals:

> British display men show little or any art knowledge about modern design or the fundamentals governing modern methods of merchandise 'presentation'.

But into the 1930s the stores were to grow in self-confidence and develop their own style of modernism. Moholy-Nagy brought his Bauhaus ideas into Simpson's of Piccadilly, John and Madeleine Duncan Miller, along with Martha Harris would transform Jaeger's, and Prudence Maufe would show 'dangerous' art at Heal's Mansard Gallery. *Harper's Bazaar* welcomed the shift in store display:

41

Doing angular things with concrete, glass and metal – so stimulating – one does give just one sigh of relief to find mahoganized, diluvian London shedding the mildew at last.

But not all London stores were swept up in this modernist fever. It was noted that Robinson & Cleaver's, which had suddenly gone modern to everyone's surprise, reneged and returned to conventionality. S.S. Sirrett, display manager at Dickins & Jones, declared against the tide:

> We are at last seeing the end of Futurism, or at least extreme Futurism, which in my opinion is something to be thankful for ... we have had whole displays so extreme in character as to create nothing in the public mind but ridicule.

Display took an equally reactionary stand when, for the Silver Jubilee celebrations, it confidently said that the general opinion was that there was no need to resort to modernism, and that the Country and the Empire, being so rich in historic associations, 'it is unnecessary to look for any abstract or obtuse themes'.

If the London stores held mixed views on modernist designs for their window display, they much more readily accepted the materials of modernism – chrome, aluminium, glass and such early plastics as cellulose, bakelite and Perspex. Selfridges was particularly enthusiastic about chromium tubes. An article in *Commercial Art* commended their progressive use of chromium:

> Steel tubes which for years past have supported in millions of bicycles millions of tons of flesh and blood, are now to the delight of the display expert properties of an entirely different, though not less useful nature.

In the 1930s chromium tubes did not hide themselves coyly under merchandise, but flaunted themselves, as one admirer put it, showing 'their beautifully rounded, highly reflective surfaces'. Aluminium sold itself to the more cautious in display as a happy medium lying between old style products and new garish

Opposite
Simpson's display window, to the design of Moholy-Nagy, 1936.

materials, as chrome. And glass, which suitably lit could prove as sparkling
as chrome, was not just used for support, but sported itself in a variety of
new forms – bricked, wired, mirrored and moulded – whilst Pilkington's
experiments with Vitroflex produced sheets of glass tiles which could be used
flexibly as screens in display. The merits and demerits of non-reflective glass for
shop windows was endlessly discussed in the display press, Shorter being one
of its main evangelists, particularly, as he would argue, 'for when the windows
were large and the merchandise lacked colour'.

Early plastics began to be used for a myriad of display accessories, from
stacked stands to coat hangers, show cards and price tickets. The advantages
of plastics in display were their flexibility and capacity for being moulded into
an infinite number of shapes, and the fact that they could be easily cleaned.
Shop-fitting firms quickly latched on to these possibilities and a number of new
supply firms came on to the scene sporting 'plastic' in their name. Mannequins,
previously largely made of wax were now made of composite materials

that maintained their colour and were unaffected by temperature changes. Incidentally the '30s brought a growth of a British mannequin industry albeit the major supplier was Schaufensterkunst, now under the disguise of British Display Figures.

Much of the technical advancements in window display were, in fact, led by the suppliers, and the same can be said for the stores' increasing preoccupation with the use of lighting in displays. Here such firms as Osram and Magda were in the fore, and electrical engineers began to feature in the display press explaining the technicalities of their products and their possible display usages, particularly the use of neon and fluorescent tubes. Such large suppliers as Levine & Sons fanfared that 'from now on neon will become more and more an integral part of the shop window'; whilst other fitters hyped the fact that 'tubes can be made to follow almost any design and will outline practically any shape'. John Lewis introduced neon lighting all along their Oxford Street frontage; and Selfridges was reported as using 3,100 feet of tube lighting. In the '30s lighting came to be appreciated not only as a means of attracting customers to a store but as an essential element in creating effects, as with Harrods in their regular display of Elizabeth Arden products. One such was described as having 'the head of Elizabeth Arden with a red light behind it, giving a soft pink glow to the head'.

The mid-30s was, of course, much taken up with Royal events, George v's Silver Jubilee [May 1935], quickly followed by his death [Jan. 1936] and George vi's Coronation [May 1937]. *Display* urged stores to be imaginative in their Jubilee windows along the lines 'the knowledge that the sun never sets on the British Empire gives the display designer a plethora of ideas'; whilst Goldsman, ex-Selfridges, now a display consultant, provided impressive articles on the history of previous displays for Royal occasions as an inspiration for projected displays. Shopfitting suppliers had timely advertisements for flags, heraldic devices, replicas of the King and Queen, giant photographs of royal sites, and similar accessories. Store windows were inevitably flooded with red, white and blue. Whiteley's actually acted as a supplier to other stores for Jubilee decorations and lighting.

Display was rather disappointed with the general standard of results:

> I was very surprised to see a comparative scarcity of enterprising Jubilee window schemes but I observed that the Jubilee theme was introduced into almost every window, although in many cases effectively but unobtrusively.

Swan & Edgar, for example, was congratulated on the 'dignity' of their display, but it was inevitable that Selfridges got the palm d'or for its splendour. Their decorations covered some 1,200 feet, of which nearly every inch was festooned with flags and plaques, topped by a gigantic figure of Britannia [82ft] designed by Sir William Reid Dick.

George v's death gave yet another opportunity for display personnel to 'show off', this time purple and black replacing red, white and blue. D.H. Evans had all its front blinds drawn except for two – the one simply draped in black with a portrait of the King in uniform, the other with just a wreath of purple tulips. Harrods, in spite of the solemnity of the occasion wanting to continue to show merchandise, added the appropriate colour, as when they posed their black millinery with mourning drapes and black and purple flowers.

Of course the display world was rather caught out with the abdication of Edward viii:

> it [the abdication] came as a very great shock at a most inconvenient time. Plans had been proceeding rapidly and which, in many cases, involved unusually large sums of capital, were suspended almost at a moments notice.

Nevertheless stores quickly realized that much of the prepared material could still be used with small amendments albeit one store was reputed to have paid a sculptor some 300gns to model Edward. With their quickness to adapt, window designers soon saw the advantage of being able to add feminine touches by including Queen Elizabeth, and even the princesses, in their displays. A later 'royal' example of quick change was, in 1939, when, overnight, Harrods changed all their windows to greet the Royal couple on their return from an American-Canadian tour.

Apart from the Royal events and the normal festive and seasonal windows, the theme that seems to have obsessed display designers in the '30s was that of outdoor and physical activities. There had always been the pursuits of the wealthy – hunting, shooting and fishing – to inspire displays, but now, with statutory holidays with pay, more of the population could 'holiday'. Increased car ownership also provided new leisure opportunities, whilst the various transport companies were active in promoting the attractions of the countryside as well as the seaside. Physical fitness was encouraged by the National Fitness Council; and organisations, such as the Rambling Association and Youth Hostel Association, gave hiking a moral dimension that paralleled the apparent hedonism and luxury of cruising and bathing in the Mediterranean.

Charles Wyld of Fortnum and Mason's, Austin Reed and Alec Simpson were all sports enthusiasts and their respective windows would show the latest fashion and equipment related to their interests; and across the London stores whole scenes would be constructed showing people picnicking [clothes, hampers and food, rugs etc.] or at the seaside or on a cruise boat. Sports equipment abounded, as with Selfridges astounding 'stunt' window with football, lacrosse and hockey accoutrements all splayed out across one window. Modernist mannequins, besporting bathing costumes, featured widely, particularly noteworthy were the ones produced by Gottwald Ltd.

The '30s that had started with *Commercial Art's* depressing comments on the state of British display, finished rather abruptly with the onset of war. Yet such progress had been made through the decade that eminent display specialists, such as Misha Black, could show a chink of optimism:

Gottwald 'sporting' mannequins, 1935.

48

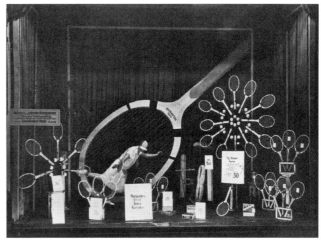

Above
Selfridges window, McKnight Kauffer, 1925.

Above right
Selfridges tennis season window.

[display] is creeping from the stage when we thought that every German display was a good one and every American display a mouthpiece to be slavishly copied, in Great Britain, British display has come of age.

Many of the London stores had experienced wartime conditions during the First World War and although this had had serious effects on retail – restricted availability of merchandise, staff enlisted into the services etc. – the conditions experienced in London in WWII were altogether more formidable. Firstly there were altogether more government restrictions as the Raw Materials Act, the Fuel Restriction Act, and clothes rationing. The Raw Materials Act, for example, banned for commercial purposes 'any advertising novelty, counter display device or window display device in relation to the sale of goods' that used paper or wood pulp.

Many stores lost their key display staff as when Austin Reed's Taylor Rose joined up. Grieve reported Harrods windows as being carried out by 15 to 18

Above
Heal's wartime window with decorated hoarding, 1941.

Above right
Austin Reed's wartime window with decorated half-hoarding, 1940s.

year old boys, [no women were employed at that time], as anyone of military age had been called up and display was not considered a protected occupation.

There were restrictions on street and store lighting and, because of the possibility of bombing, store windows began to be boarded up or crisscrossed with gummed tape to prevent splintering. Grieve considered all of this as a glass half full and saw such constraints as a spur to ingenuity. A lead was given by the Building Centre which, with the co-operation of the government Register of Designers, mounted an exhibition in 1941 showing how to protect glass and merchandise from the effects of bombing yet manage to make an attractive display of goods at the same time.

Some London stores totally boarded certain windows, others part-boarded them or had boarding with 'peep-holes', through which goods could be seen. Some stores, as Heals, took the opportunity to cover their boarding with advertisements, whilst some even decorated the sand bags, protecting their frontages, to attract customers' attention. It is reported that one store actually made a feature of the patterns it constructed with brown tape and had a ticket as to how the tape could be bought and for how much!

Initially most stores tried to continue their displays as they would have normally done, before the war – 'white sales', Easter bunnies and the like – demonstrating Grieve's attitude to things:

> War is a depressing thought, and the window gazer wants to be cheered up
> and reminded of the pleasantest side of life.

And the not-disinterested Association of Display Producers and Silk Screen Printers similarly urged their customers – the stores – along the lines 'Let's be positive'. But very soon the seriousness of the situation became obvious and a more confronting patriotic stand was taken, both because it was sincerely felt and seriously needed, but also because, cynically, it made commercial sense. Soon the London stores were competing fiercely as to which could be seen to be contributing most to the war effort.

'Useful' merchandise began to replace 'fashionable', or what had been previously displayed as the 'latest thing'; and the utilitarian aspects of merchandise began to be focused on. Goods suitable for periods in air raid shelters appeared. D.H. Evans sold sleeping bags, as Jaeger had sold its camel-hair ones in WWI; trousers for women now on war work were featured; and such novelties as the all-in-one siren suit, popularized by Churchill, became the fashion. As in WWI some stores were designated producers of uniforms. A typical Austin Reed advertisement exploited this:

> Good clothes, faultless tailoring and absolute correctness of detail are in
> every Austin Reed coat whether it be of the 'great' or 'over' variety.

Soon store windows were being devoted entirely to patriotic themes – Harrods featured some of Doris Zinkeisen's pictures of war injuries on behalf of the Red Cross and St. John's Fund; Marshall & Snelgrove had 'Free French' displays; D.H. Evans had its windows filled with quotes from Churchill's most rousing

Whiteley's wartime propaganda window, 1940.

speeches; Selfridges put on an Allied Naval display and Whiteley's similarly featured one on the Merchant Navy; whilst Peter Robinson's had relief maps showing the position of the Allied armies; examples are myriad.

But all of this was taken to a more intense level, and standardized, when the Ministry of Information offered to supply to the stores whole displays on propaganda themes, with the proviso that windows in which these appeared should not have store merchandise in them at the same time. The Ministry issued fortnightly lists of themes for which they would make material available – maps, posters, and, particularly, photo-enlargements. These were issued ten days before the display was to be mounted, with the condition that it should last at least six days. The very first scheme was entitled 'Hold fast and we win'. Typical of the Ministry's themes is a selection of some issued between July and December in 1942:

'Immunisation against diptheria'
'Storage of vegetables for winter'
'Fuel economy'
'Wise spending of clothing coupons'
'Don't travel more than you must – war needs come first'
'Trap that mouse'
'Post early for Christmas'

Although stores were to complain about the quality of much of the Ministry of Information material, the Ministry employed first rate people to produce it, as F.H.K. Henrion for 'Life-Line' on the Merchant Navy; the designer de Holden Stone for 'The March of a Nation' on u.s. aid; and George Orwell for 'Free Europe' forces' on allied troops.

Not only were store windows given over to the war effort but parts of the stores themselves. Most London stores had air-raid shelters in their basements and Simpson's set aside a space for a servicemen's club [as Selfridges had done in wwi]; some stores still had floors occupied by government agencies through to the late '40s.

The 'home front' contribution of display personnel did much to strengthen their position. The New Year edition of *Display* in 1947 pronounced optimistically:

To-day, no-one with anything to sell, from a bag of peanuts to a political theory, can afford to forget that display is the medium most directly concerned with selling.

Although the government ministries may well have been completely sold on the importance of display to get their various messages across, many store owners were yet to be persuaded of the importance of allotting an increased proportion of their budgets to their windows. And, practically, stores were still faced with scarcity of materials and government restrictions in the post-war years of austerity. Most were involved with reconstruction after wartime bombing; many still reglazing their windows, as Waring & Gillows and Liberty's, well after the war had ended. And even when reconstruction was completed there was a shortage of consumer goods to display and the quality of much that was available was hardly of the quality to inspire those who were obliged to make the best of what they received.

Stafford Bourne, the Director of Bourne & Hollingsworth summarized the situation facing most London stores:

> It is practically impossible to repair windows, obtain adequate display equipment, and keep the inside of the windows decorated; and, in any case, with out artificial lighting good display is impossible.

Lighting regulations were not relaxed until the late Spring of 1949 when stores sprang into action, and even managements seemed prepared to make additional investments for at least the lighting aspects of their windows. Austin Reeds splashed out, in celebration, floodlighting the whole of their building in amber.

A major post-war government concern was to boost exports, so restricted during the war – to aim for a better balance of trade – and many London stores decided to contribute to this national drive, in a similar way as to their wartime spirit. The Regent Street Association settled on using 'export' as the theme of their 21st birthday celebrations in 1947. Gillian Crawshay Williams, Jaeger's display manager, was particular commended all round for her 'export' windows with 'balance of trade' scales showing Jaeger clothes being exported balanced by cut-outs of meat, sugar and other essentials, of necessity having to be imported; she extended the theme to the interior of the store with additional explanations of the country's need, as well as flaunting the store's exterior with related banners.

54

Peter Robinson, display of Dannimacs, 1951.

Although the appreciation of the 'Swinging London' youth market was not really in full flood until the turn of the '50s into the '60s with such as Bazaar on the King's Road and Marion Foale and Sally Tuffin in Carnaby Street, some London stores were beginning to turn to youth in their window displays during the 1950s. Both Heal's and Liberty's set out to attract young home buyers, largely those with 'taste' and well-lined pockets, by importing exciting new designs from the Continent which had been impossible during the war years. Heal's had particularly strong contacts with Scandinavia, and their windows were full of the latest designs in glass, china and furniture; Liberty's shrugging off, or possibly putting on a back burner, their arts and crafts tradition, had windows flaunting such radical Italian designers as Gio Ponti and Paoli Venini, as well as the young British designer Robin Day.

During the 1950s the two display giants, Selfridges and Harrods were largely preoccupied with boardroom battles with Charles Clore and Hugh Fraser respectively, so that 'Miss Selfridge' and 'Way In' were not launched until well into the '60s; whilst Austin Reeds and Simpsons, not so preoccupied, nevertheless did not launch their 'Cue' range and 'Young Simpson' mini-shop, again until the late '60s. Dickins & Jones, however, had understood the potentiality of youthful consumers as early as 1947 when they opened their 'Young Londoner' department. And Jaeger, also stole a march on the others when it appointed Jean Muir and her then assistant, David Watts, [still a student at the Royal College of Arts] to design their 'Boutique' range, which attracted the younger customer to their windows.

Simpson's display window, 1952.

Selfridges window, McKnight Kauffer, 1925.

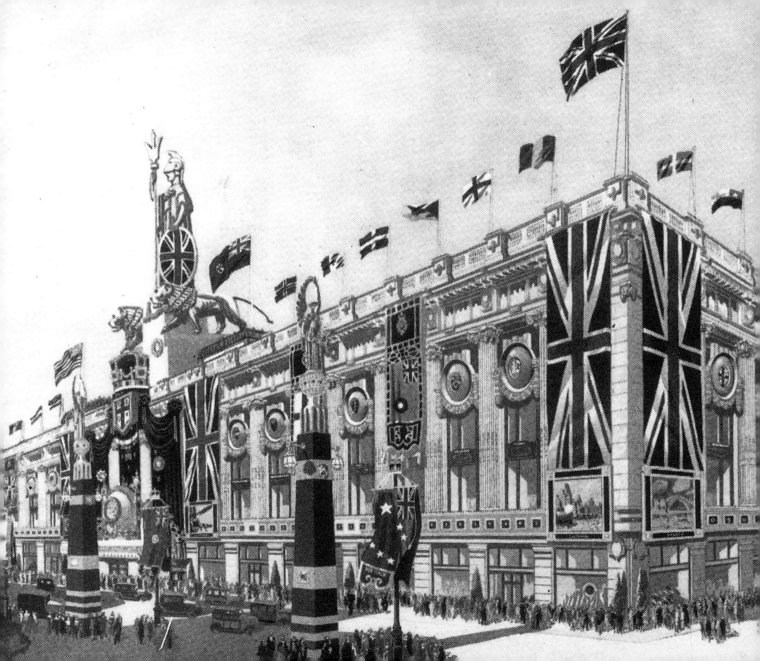

SHOWING OFF

THE EVENTS

In 1925 a news item in *Display* commented on one of Gordon Selfridge's 'stunts':

> Some would attempt to point out that they were not merchandising show. Maybe that is true for in a strict sense of the word they were not, but they succeeded in getting record crowds not only to come to the store but inside the store too.

Of course, all the London stores put on merchandising 'events' through the year – seasonal offerings, Christmas and Easter shows, and sales. A typical sales notice was that for Debenham & Freebody's in 1921:

> Messrs. Debenham & Freebody, of Wigmore Street, open their sale this morning and it will last to Saturday week. They offer furs and silks at half price, and tempting bargains in many other departments … They state explicitly that no goods have been purchased specially for the sale.

White sales were particularly popular, Harrods, one year, astounding its customers by having coloureds in a white sale. But most stores would, from time to time, have irregular 'events' as bringing in crafts people on site to demonstrate how certain goods had been produced, as, for example, Pontings did for their handbags. Fashion shows were particularly popular, especially crowd pulling if a society 'name' could be attached, as when Selfridge had Lady Furness and her twin sister, Gloria Vanderbilt, stage and model one. Furniture stores would similarly put on special events, as Liberty's had done in the 1880s when they constructed a complete house to show off their Far Eastern merchandise, and then, in the 1950s whole room sets to show off their Italian imports.

However, 'events', taking more the form of 'stunts', were a rather different way of 'showing off', not by finding new ways of displaying the store's merchandise, but by staging 'happenings' that would, by association, add kudos to the store's reputation. Banquets and parties had been used as

A fashion show at Whiteleys, 1934.

Above
Lunch at the Café Royal celebrating the opening of Austin Reed's Regent Street store, 1926.

Above right
Harrods 'white' sale, including poodles, marking the visit of the French President to London, 1939.

publicity by stores since the mid-19th century when William Whiteley, in spite of his unpopularity, would gather round him the great and the good from the City and from Parliament. It became customary for stores to have celebratory meals when a new building had been completed as, for example, when Austin Reed held a lunch at the Café Royal, opposite his new store, with, as honoured guest, Sir Reginald Blomfield, who had largely been responsible for the redevelopment of Regent Street. And, similarly, when the new Derry & Tom's building was opened in 1933, amongst its 250 guests were Gordon Selfridge, Sir Woodman Burbidge of Harrods, Austin Reed and Eric Gamage of Gamages. Of course, it was essential that the press received a detailed account of such feasts, particularly of the most celebrated names attending – the more distinguished the guest list, the more improved the store's image.

But when Gordon Selfridge arrived, with all the razzle dazzle of a circus ringmaster, 'feasting' went up a notch or two. Amongst the dozens of banquets and social events he was to give over the years the most noteworthy were his

General Election parties, of which he had six. These would inevitably become all night affairs, with large 'state of the poll' scoreboards showing results as they came in. And although there would always be a sprinkle of City and governmental worthies attending, Selfridge's guests would tend to have the glamour of theatreland and the cinema, including such personalities as Gladys Cooper and Charlie Chaplin.

And it was Selfridge who appreciated the fascination the public had for new inventions. History has it that within a few days of his hearing that Blériot had crossed the Channel, he had the very plane on show in his store:

> This flight was so big I had to link it to the store, I saw some sort of omen in
> it. Blériot and I were changing the world, each in our own way.

This Selfridge prank was subsequently followed over the years by displays of wireless telegraphy, x-ray, a 'talkie' film set, and so on. Even the reluctant Baird was inveigled to demonstrate his embryonic television equipment. Flying was the rage – Harrods began to sell flying lessons as well as planes, and Simpson's too hoisted planes into its new Piccadilly store, with Moholy-Nagy designing an accompanying aviation exhibition. Simpson's stunts were to become altogether more 'sporty'.

Simpson's store could be said to have been founded on sport, with DAKS trousers being designed in order that enthusiastic golfers, which included Alec Simpson, should not have to wear braces on the golf course. *The Field* hyped Simpson's as the 'sportsman's paradise', selling clothes and accessories for a vast number of outdoor activities from fly fishing to polo. So in order to sell his clothes Simpson went all out to attract as many sports stars to the store, as Selfridge had done with actors and film stars. 'Stunts' would be to show Queen Victoria and Albert's skating boots or Gordon Richards' riding boots. In 1948 Simpson's played host to overseas athletes attending the London Olympic Games. The store always tried to have keen sportsmen to head its sports centre with the likes of Ronnie Curson, who would bring along his

Selfridges celebrating the Coronation
of Queen Elizabeth, 1952.

Princess Margaret attending a charity ball, Selfridges, 1952.

tennis friends, Gardner Molloy and Budge Patty, and his successor, John Palmer, bringing in the next tennis generation of Rosewall and Hoad.

Liberty's, not known for any 'sportiness', curiously became associated with horse racing with its Derby Day scarf. This was an annual stunt when a scarf, illustrating some aspect of racing, would be set up for printing with a gap for the name of that year's winner. A manager would rush the name of the winner to the Merton works to be printed in the gap so quickly that Epsom race goers could buy a scarf on the way home.

Harrods was also wont to put on 'events'. Having the largest piano showroom in London it became particularly known for musical 'stunts' as laying on orchestral concerts, its first being in 1909, with the likes of

A LOYAL TRIBUTE

This distinctive display at Harrods was a particularly tasteful tribute. No merchandise or advertising matter was included in the scheme.

Sir Thomas Beecham and Sir Henry Wood bringing in their respective orchestras to the store for free concerts. The store would have leading soloists give recitals – Noël Coward entertained customers in the piano department and Victor Sylvester played for tea dances. And Harrods would sponsor musical events as when it supported a touring opera group. The midday tour of the store by a Scottish bagpiper at the turn of the 21st century can perhaps be considered the end of a much shrunken line traceable back to such glories.

'Showing off' events that might build reputations through philanthropy, were exploited to the full by most of the London stores. Burbidge, at Harrods, played the charity card to the full when, in 1895, Harrods responded to a Daily Telegraph campaign to collect money for 'Christmas dinners for Cripples' with its vans at the ready to distribute hampers for the cause. Of course food giving was always Fortnum & Mason's forte when it came to charity, with hampers for Wellington's troops, beef tea for Florence Nightingale's patients and Christmas puddings for 20th century prisoners-of-war. Selfridges was not to be outdone on the charity front, and beyond such stunts as getting a handful of titled ladies to serve behind its counters to raise money for 'training schools for mothers in the East End', it was particularly active with war charities. Examples are a number of events it mounted in WWI to raise money for such causes as King Albert's Belgian Relief Fund, the Russian Relief Fund, and the Serbian Red Cross. Selfridge was particularly smugly triumphant when he got half a dozen Royals, including the then Duke and Duchess of York to a banquet to raise money for hospital building.

Events associating a store with Royalty were to be generally exploited as a means of 'showing off'. Of the myriad of examples is Trevor Bowen of Barkers, who had risen from being their pastry chef to general management, but who returned to his trade, in 1922, to bake the wedding cake for the marriage of Princess Mary to Viscount Lascelles. The cake received tremendous press coverage being some seven and a half feet high and festooned with Greek temples and goddesses, along with the relevant coats of arms. And both

Opposite left
Harrods' 'tasteful' tribute to George V, 1936.

Opposite right
Wedding cake presented to the Princess Royal baked by Trevor Bowen, Chairman of John Barker's, 1921.

Below
Austin Reed's window display for
Ashes series, 1932.

Selfridges and Barkers [at Derry & Toms' roof garden], kept records of royal visitors as well as notables from stage and screen – Selfridges on a panel that it got its visitors to write on, and Barkers in visitors books, later presented to the local archives.

ENGLAND v AUSTRALIA

Typical advertisement by supplier for accessories,
Coronation of George VI, 1937.

One of Simpson's annual Christmas Tree
of lights by Natasha Kroll, 1950s.

SHOWING OFF
THE CATALOGUES

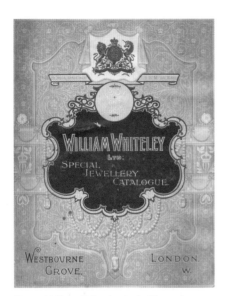

Cover, William Whiteley Ltd., 'Special Jewellery Catalogue', 1901–02.

Previous page
Close-up crop of cover, John Lewis, 'Monthly Special Notices', 1932.

Opposite left
Liberty catalogue, 1912, tea gown in 'Nirvana silk crape'.

Opposite right
Cover, Peter Jones catalogue, 1926.

From the second half of the 19th century London stores found an alternative way of 'showing off' their wares in addition to placing them in their windows; this was to have pictures, descriptions, types of their merchandise sent out to prospective customers by mail in booklet or catalogue format. Harrods produced its first catalogue in 1870, Jaeger in 1877. The catalogue became to be considered an essential sales medium for such classy stores as Harrods, Fortnum & Mason and Liberty's, all of which had customers living out-of-town, only occasionally actually visiting the store; whilst those of the Army & Navy Store were living in the far flung parts of the British Empire and had an even greater need to know what was available. As late as 1939 the Army & Navy's catalogue/price list ran to over one thousand pages, and included goods for most overseas emergencies – building materials, portable toilets, rifles – everything down to memorial stones.

Catalogues took a variety of forms, of shapes and sizes and methods of reproducing images of merchandise, from weighty price lists as for Harrods, Whiteleys and the Army & Navy, largely carrying information with little room for hype, to more focused specialized catalogues or even leaflets on a particular department's goods or even one specific line – corsets seem to have been a popular choice in the 1910s and 1920s! Then there would be seasonal issues, jogging customers' memories as to their possible oncoming Christmas needs, or that Spring was on its way, or that Summer holidays needed to be provided for. And a number of stores would send out catalogues or lists for special celebrations, as Simpson's lavish brochure for the Festival of Britain.

Some of the early London store catalogues not only presented the merchandise in as attractive a way as possible, given reproductive methods of the time, but had perforated pages which could be torn out and returned to the store with the customers' added instructions for ordering. The picturesque ladies' fashion catalogues for Liberty's, pre-WWI, were divided into two sections – 'costumes never out of fashion' and 'novelties for the season', with each garment given a name. The 'never out of fashion' robes had such

OLD ENGLISH.
Ena. Tea Gown, in Nirvana
silk-crape, with panel and
sleeves of Dalghali silk-crape.
Silk embroidery. 25 guineas

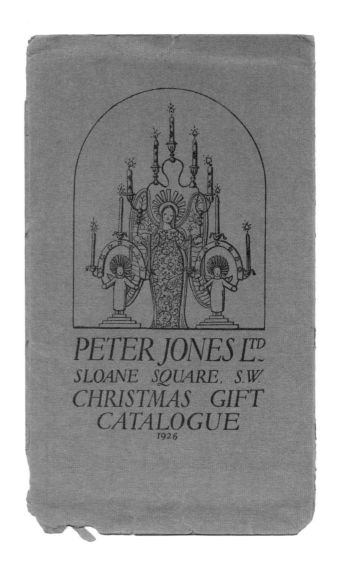

PETER JONES LTD
SLOANE SQUARE, S.W.
CHRISTMAS GIFT
CATALOGUE
1926

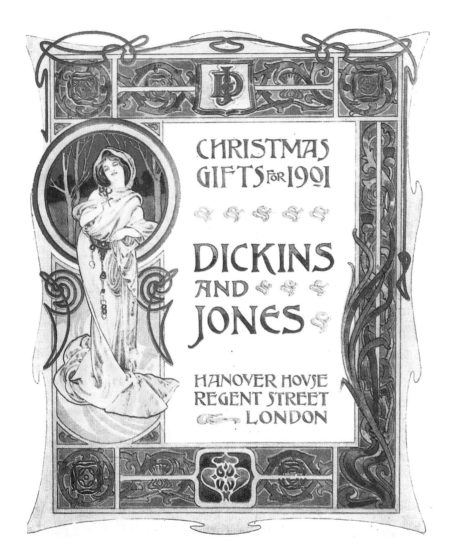

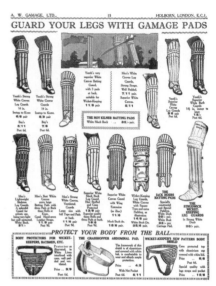

Gamage's Sports catalogue, 'Guard your legs with Gamage pads', undated, c.1920s.

Left
Cover, Dickins & Jones Christmas catalogue, 1901.

Advertisement for whisky in Army & Navy general price list, 1939–40.

historical names as Eleanore and Herce, the 'novelties for the season' such curiosities as Olga and Mercia. The customers were asked to tear out the appropriate page:

> Dresses can be made to any design desired IF SUGGESTIONS ARE SENT DESCRIBING WHAT IS WANTED, and variations can be made to any of the models illustrated in this book.

This tendency to give some merchandise names rather than numbers seems to have continued right through to the 1950s for a Derry & Toms catalogue of that period offers suites of furniture with such names as 'Somerset' and 'Edinburgh'.

Many catalogues had lengthy hypes for certain products or took the opportunity to extol the reputation of their business or the grandeur of their property. An early Whiteley's catalogue in addition to an extensive price list [with the curious appendage 'the prices in this list are subject to fluctuations in the market'] 'showed off' the buoyant state of the store's finances:

> Owing to the vast increase of business ... we have found it necessary to extend our Show Rooms, which are now fitted in the very best style. These rooms are 140 ft long by 35 ft wide; and are splendidly lighted to show off the goods to advantage.

And Jaeger catalogues continued to contain lengthy diatribes in praise of Gustav Jaeger and the advantages of wearing animal rather than plant products, although these homilies did lighten and shorten over the years.

For the early store catalogues thousands of product images of necessity were reproduced by meticulous black and white drawings or etchings or scraperboard with colour only gradually being introduced, and photographic reproduction only being used to any great extent well into the inter-war years.

When it came to catalogue design Heal's led the way. Ambrose Heal, a designer himself, and one of the founders of the Design & Industries

Cover, Jaeger ladieswear catalogue, 1928.

Cover, Peter Robinson catalogue, c.1924.

AT
HEAL'S

196, TOTTENHAM COURT ROAD
LONDON, W. 1.

Cover, Heal's catalogue, 1929,
illust. Herry Perry.

Association [DIAS] in 1915, was one of the first to use well known artists and copywriters such as commissioning covers from the likes of McKnight Kauffer and Herry Perry in the 1920s, and copy from Noel Carrington in the 1930s. Heal's catalogue covers frequently besported designs from DIA members. From 1929 Austin Reed's actually produced a disguised sales booklet in magazine form for its customers – *Modern Man* – which had had attractive modernist covers, unsigned. Jaeger were using the distinguished Vogue fashion illustrator Francis Marshall for its sales leaflets from about 1939, and after WWII commissioned covers from André François and the renowned René Gruau.

And then there was Fortnum & Mason [F&M], which stood apart from all other London stores when it came to catalogues. F&M had been producing sales literature from as early as 1817, but it was Hugh Stuart Menzies, a department head as well as responsible for the store's advertising, who was to radically change their publications when he left to found the Stuart Advertising Agency with the store now as his client.

> I visualized little booklets sent to a carefully chosen mailing list; booklets as readable as something bought at a bookstall or drawn from a library. Every preconceived notion of a trade catalogue was to be violated. Space was to be sacrificed to pure fun in every direction.

The early 'new-style' catalogues were written by Stuart Menzies himself and illustrated by W.M. Hendy, amongst others. Peyton Skipworth in his entertaining book on later Fortnum & Mason publications quotes a description by Stuart Menzies of the store's turtle soup:

> When we speak of Turtle Soup our voice becomes very tender – do not think us unmanly. We have in mind the spiced Turtle Soup for those who feast regally …

Stores had never seen anything like such gaiety in a catalogue. And this vein continued when Edward Bawden became the main illustrator for Fortnum's, first working with Stuart Menzies, and then, after WWII with Ruth Gill, and her copywriter Lilla Spicer of Colman, Prentis & Varley. Robert Harling wrote of Bawden's relationship with Stuart Menzies, 'His drawings were exactly attuned to Menzies' almost carefree yet cunningly persuasive prose.' And later Mary Gowing wrote of Bawden's relationship with Ruth Gill:

> Bawden was a perfect partner and counterpoise to her, her clean typography contrasting with and yet complementing, his strongly defined drawings…

Debenhams, Model Gowns catalogue, c.1930s.

Cover, Derry & Toms catalogue, 1933, illus. Michael Wellmer.

Fortnum & Mason leaflet,
illus. Edward Bawden, 1937.

Fortnum & Mason Christmas Catalogue,
illus. Edward Bawden, 1958.

Cover, Harvey Nichols' Christmas catalogue, 1929.

GRANTA 4 Gns.
A slim-fitting model
made easy to wear in
stock-size by the sash
tying at the back.
In Genita (a kind of
Jersey-de-Soie). Green,
Sapphire or Black.
Size 40 ins. (hips).

GORDON 79/6
In Jersey-de-Soie with
a softly gathered bodice
and cut on flowing lines.
In Black/White, Black/
Red, Navy/White,
Brown/Rust.
Sizes 40, 42 ins. (hips).

MALTA 6½ Gns.
A sleeveless Dress and
Jacket adapted from a
model by Patou. In
several designs of Blue
and White printed
Crepe-de-Chine.
Size 40 ins. (hips).

JOHN LEWIS
AND COMPANY LIMITED

1932   MONTHLY SPECIAL NOTICES   **JUNE**
These Monthly Special Notices are sent Free on request.

Cover, John Lewis, 'Monthly Special Notices', 1932.

John Lewis, 'Summer Gazette', 1940.

Cover, 'Harrods News', 1955.

SHOWING OFF THE ADVERTISING

'If you are willing to humbug people you can do a quite effective amount of what is called advertising for a charge on your profits …'

'The Chinese are inclined to take opium – the British retailers are inclined to advertise.'

Both of these quotes come from John Spedan Lewis of John Lewis, who saw advertising as largely a costly drain with little proven effect on sales. William Whiteley had had much the same attitude as Mr. Lewis, refusing 'to pay for space in the vulgar company of his rivals in the advertisement pages'. Nevertheless Whiteley was not adverse to using the Press to gain publicity through editorials extolling his achievements. Eventually he decided to publish his own newspaper – the *Westbourne Gazette & Belgravia Herald*. This proved a disaster, failing within six months, its decline helped along, not unexpectedly, by unfavourable comments in the rival local paper, the *Bayswater Chronicle*.

But the Lewises and the Whiteleys were in the minority, for most other London stores were tempted, at times, to spend, quite happily, large parts of their budgets on advertising, with a carefree unbounded optimism. Harrods put out their first press advertisements in the Pall Mall Gazette in 1866; Peter Robinson was advertising from 1874; and Heal's were probably one of the earliest, starting in the 1840s. Their archive records show that by the mid-1920s

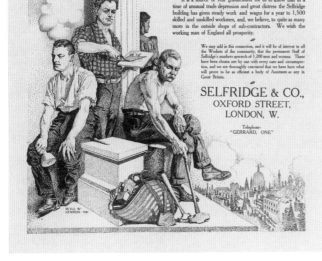

Selfridges poster fanfaring rapid construction of its store, 1908.

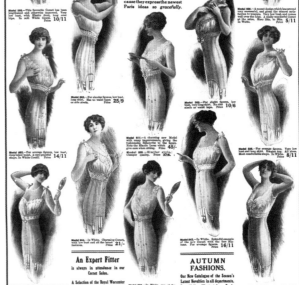

Barker's corset advertisement in *The Queen*, 1913.

Swan & Edgar, advertisement of its 'good taste' gowns – 'Brighton', 'Greville' and 'Ascot', 1913.

not only were they using posters and press advertisements, but circulars, 10,000 being place in one issue of *The Connoisseur*.

Gordon Selfridge was very far from shunning press advertising; rather he embraced it with energy and enthusiasm. Gordon Honeycombe wrote of Selfridge's viewpoint:

> He not only opened up a bottomless income for the papers, pouring thousands of pounds into their coffers himself, he showed other stores and businesses a way to wealth through advertising, and gave to the advertising industry both impetus and new directions, and helped to turn it into an art.

Whilst his store was still being constructed Selfridge was regularly feeding the press with news of the wonder of the building's construction, with such hyping as, in November 1908, 'we have broken all previous building records, and that without any overtime of any consequence …'. He placed two column advertisements, resembling editorials, in the *Times*, in the weeks leading up to the store's opening, and was wont to include the names of 'personalities' in his advertising, aiming to gain kudos by association. Harrods, most notoriously, employed this style of advertising when it placed full-paged advertisements containing screeds, apparently from the pens of the likes of Arnold Bennett and Bernard Shaw, actually drawn from letters from the two turning down Harrods' suggestion for them to become involved in the stores' publicity.

From 1912 Selfridge went on to use covert advertising, resembling journalistic articles, under the heading of Calisthenes, the first one being entitled 'On the Joy of Learning'. The Calisthenes features appeared regularly in national and evening newspapers, including the *Daily Telegraph*, the *Daily Mail* and the *Times*. These, apparent articles, became so popular that a selection were published in book form as early as 1916, and again in 1933. Selfridge claimed that Calisthenes 'had been the first man ever attached formally and officially to a great enterprise to write about it …' Fortnum & Mason was

Swan & Edgar, advertisement showing its building, *c.* early-1900s.

Harrods, advertisement in *The Playgoer*, 1910.

Harrods, advertisement for military uniforms, 1917.

Derry & Toms, winter sale advertisement, illus. McKnight Kauffer.

similarly to advertise through 'commentaries' written by Stuart Menzies of the Stuart Advertising Agency.

From the First World War most of the London stores began to adopt a favourite advertising agency, and along with it its designers and artists – Army & Navy used Stuarts as did Fortnum & Mason, which later on changed to Colman, Prentis Varley [CPV]; Bourne & Hollingsworth used Notley Advertising, Harvey Nichols used Samson Clark & Osborne Peacock, Heals used Pritchard Wood & Partners, and so on. A few agencies worked for a number of stores, presumably not experiencing any conflict of interest, as CPV who provided designs and copy for Dickens & Jones, D.H. Evans, Jaeger and Fortnum & Mason. Sir Woodman Burbidge of Harrods, looking back from 1944, declared that his store had always done their own advertising but there are instances when they also used outside agencies.

The two stores, starting out as men's outfitters, that had some of the most successful advertising campaigns were Austin Reed's, from the 1920s, and Simpson's of Piccadilly, from the mid-30s. Austin Reed's were advertising their own products – the Stanaust shirt and the Summit shirt and collar from the turn of the century. *The Advertising World* wrote of it:

> Mr. Reed's advertising … is uniformly of the best quality – in ideas and appearance – and is among the 'liveliest', most attractive and thoroughly done advertising we have seen issued by any retailer.

Percy Epps, Reed's advertising manager, saw that the store was not only constantly mentioned in the Press, but was advertised on the Underground. Epps was succeeded by W.D.H. McCullough who, when he left to join Pritchard Wood & Partners, took the Austin Reed account with him and ran it for some twelve years to 1937. Austin Reed's was to continue to use the agency through to the 1950s.

When the Austin Reed flagship store opened in Regent Street in 1926 they ran a press and poster campaign with such slogans as 'Men about Regent Street' and 'New Tailoring'. Through the inter-war years the store's advertisements appeared regularly in the *Radio Times*, *Punch* and similar national magazines. And in WWII its slogans were suitably patriotically slanted to 'On Active Service' and 'With the Fleet'.

Each store inevitably used the artists retained or employed by its respective advertising agency, and although other artists would work for Austin Reed from time to time, from campaign to campaign, as, for example, Austin Cooper, Eckersley-Lombers and Fougasse [who provided cartoons from 1937 through to 1948], it was Tom Purvis who was their most prolific. Between 1925

Harvey Nichols, winter sale advertisement, *Illustrated London News*, 1924.

Swan & Edgar, 'Xmas' advertisement, illus. Terence Prentis, 1927.

Austin Reed, advertisement, illus. Tom Purvis, 1927.

Austin Reed, advertisement, illus.
Tom Purvis, 1928.

and 1941 Purvis, a Camberwell trained artist, carried out over five hundred different designs for the store, both for press and poster campaigns. During McCullough's time he would write the copy first and then get Purvis to provide the illustrations to complement the text. About his approach Purvis maintained that:

> a good poster should not puzzle people, it should be like a boxer's punch – straight, hard and quick – and should deliver the message in a flash.

In *Commercial Art* [1929], McCullough wrote of Purvis:

> Probably the height of superb simplicity in modern men's wear art is attained in the Underground posters by Tom Purvis … these form an almost perfect expression of the artistic policy of the firm. They are true, simple, sincere, arresting and charming.

Purvis developed a modernistic style, advanced for store advertising in the 1920s, using flat areas of colour, adjoining each other, without any dividing line.

Alec Simpson's advertising campaign, to launch his Piccadilly store in 1936, had a budget that ran into millions in its first year alone. On Thursday 30th April 1936 there were advertisements across national morning newspapers and London evening papers announcing the store's opening; and throughout the first year the Press was saturated with more than one hundred advertisements 'showing off' the name Simpson. Mass Observation was commissioned to report on the campaign's impact. Tom Harrison, Mass Observation's Director wrote:

> We found that the advertising for DAKS trousers and Simpson's clothes has done more to change working man's idea of clothes in this country than any one influence.

As Purvis was to serve Austin Reed's from the 1920s, so would Ashley Havinden, Art Director of Crawford's Advertising Agency, and Max Hoff

Heal's, furniture advertisement, illus. R.P. Gossop, 1928.

Liberty's, scarf advertisement, illus. Joyce Dennys, 1930s.

Jaeger sports clothes, advertisement, 1930.

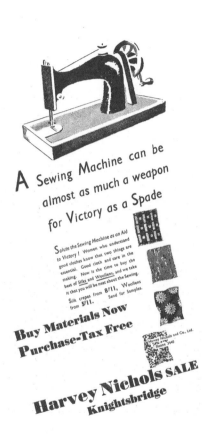

Harvey Nichols, wartime advertisement for dress-making materials.

Harrods, advertisement for Leda brand stockings, *Vogue*, 1938.

Right
Simpson's, wartime advertisement
for 'shelter suits', illus. Hoff.

What you need in an air raid

The Simpson tailored shelter suit—good looking and practical in every way. Slipped on as one garment in half a jiffy. Trousers detachable from the coat. In soft warm fleece — navy and natural. Price 70/- for men.
For women 69/6.
With a hood 82/6.

Simpson
PICCADILLY
REGENT 2002

Simpson's, DAKS advertisement,
Ashley Havinden, 1959.

Christmas advertisement showing Liberty's rebranding, Ashley Havinden, 1948.

[Maximilian Hofbauer], the fashion illustrator, work with Simpson's from the 1930s. Alec Simpson had seen Hoff's work in the *International Textile* magazine and had brought him over to London, where he was to illustrate practically all the store's advertising, both for men's and for women's wear. Hoff's illustrations, unlike those of Purvis, showed considerable detail, down to a flower in a buttonhole and the patterning of a cravat. Havinden said of Simpson's continuous use of Hoff:

> Even the artist to do the illustrations in the advertising was settled – since the visual atmosphere of a company's advertising is considerably affected by the consistent use of a given artist's style of work.

With his work at Simpson's Havinden can be said to have been the precursor of what later became known as 'corporate identity'. He insisted that there should be a 'company handwriting', which he described in the Penrose Annual for 1955:

> … from the factory itself to the product, its packaging, posters, advertisements, print matter, letter-heads, exhibitions, window displays, even down to the price tags, should be so coordinated as to present to the world a consistent, attractive appearance.

Havinden's marvellous multi-coloured typography for DAKS, and the different toned S and P of Simpson [the P serving also as the P for Piccadilly], and later on his capital L for Liberty's [starred or spotted], both appearing everywhere on everything to do with its respective store, were the essence of the store's 'handwriting'. Havinden's insistence on store 'handwriting' had the incidental spin-off of strengthening the position of window display which gradually became part of the overall presentation of a store, some display appointments coming to bridge all aspects of 'showing off', as with that of Eric Lucking at Liberty's.

Most London stores reviewed their advertising post-WWII, many deciding on a relaunch of image. Stuarts, who had done such impressive work with Fortnum & Mason's in the early inter-war years, ran the advertising account for

Autumn means...

JAEGER

Only the brave deserve the fair

and the fair deserve

JAEGER

Above
Jaeger advertisement, illus. René Gruau.

Right
Jaeger wartime advertisement,
illus. Francis Marshall.

D.H. Evan's poster, designed by CPV art director Arpad Elfer, 1955.

the Army & Navy Stores from 1949. Mass Observation was commissioned to determined the target for the campaign. As a result the advertisements extolled the accessibility of the store, being near Victoria, and its considerable range of merchandise – copy was along the lines 'Everything for Everyone – from an elephant leg stool to a darning needle'. The store went for what they described as a 'lively but dignified style', which tended to make their campaigns rather humdrum in contrast to what was going on at Jaeger's and D.H. Evans.

Jaeger retained CPV and its Creative Director Arped Elfer for its post-war campaigns. Elfer had worked with Crawford's in Paris, which had been housed in the Vogue building. For Jaeger, Elfer was to make use of some of

D.H. Evan's poster, Arpad Elfer, 1957.

Dickins & Jones' iconic emblem, designed
by René Gruau, 1953.

his old *Vogue* contacts, most frequently, at this time, René Gruau and Francis Marshall. There was nothing fine-lined about Gruau's illustrations for Jaeger's advertisements; in a few strokes he could convey the utmost glamour, even sensuality, hardly a quality previously associated with Jaeger's woolly wares. Francis Marshall had worked with *Vogue* in Paris and in London for some ten years, before becoming freelance. He actually appears to have done some illustrations for Jaeger pre-WWII, but in the post-war years was to illustrate their advertisements through the 1950s. His images were a shade more 'natural' than Gruau's, with his backgrounds suggesting more a middle-class country life style compared to Gruau's jet-setting.

CPV were also used for D.H. Evan's post-war 'fashion-wise' campaigns, targeting young women from eighteen to twenty-five. The D.H. Evan's posters, many making use of photography, flooded the Underground in the post-war years. Mary Gowing, writing of Elfer's work in *Art & Industry* remarked on the unique quality of his work for D.H. Evans:

> This advertising has the breath of life in it. It is gay, spontaneous, exciting and friendly. It has none of the debilitating too-familiar signs of compromise, because it expresses a policy that is agreed between agency and client.

SHOWING OFF
DISPLAY
PERSONNEL

Although much has been written about London store entrepreneurs, particularly about the self-publicising Gordon Selfridge, a good deal of delving was necessary to build up even rough sketches of the more active of the multitude of other personalities who contributed to London store 'showing off' of the period – the window display staff, the shopfitting companies, the display consultants and the advertising and publicity men and women.

Display personnel, although adept at 'showing off' their merchandise, seem to have been altogether less successful when it came to flaunting their own reputations. A collective effort was made by the British Association of Display Men, from 1924, [how archaic this title sounds now, but how accurate of display staff at the time], but its history was checkered. Local groups sprouted up over the country but these seem to have largely operated independently of the parent body. By the 1930s a greater unification of display men and women, appears to have been achieved, and the name had been changed, perhaps significantly, to the National Display Association [NDA].

The trade journal *Display* did much to urge an increased co-operation for professionalism with such editorials as:

> … the greater the number bound in union for the common good of professional advancement and prestige, the sooner it will be reached.

And the embryonic professional body, itself, began to take out full page advertisements, such as one entitled 'Are you getting Anywhere?', calling for increased membership, not only for general support from colleagues, but for the educational advantage of exchanging ideas. Annual national conventions were launched, and display competitions began to be held, along with such local branch activities as lectures and demonstrations. *Display* continued its efforts adding a stick to its previous carrot with such admonitions as 'you're selfish, small-minded and parochial, if you don't unite nationally'.

But 'selfish small-mindedness' seems to have prevailed as in 1934 NDA was disbanded. Although it was reformed a couple of years later it seems to have

Are You Getting Anywhere?

DON'T BE LIKE THE SQUIRREL—
ceaselessly toiling but getting NOWHERE

DON'T make the mistake of trying to plod along in your work without getting the education and expert knowledge of the DISPLAY MEN in the best positions.

One man will settle down into the routine of his calling, digging the ruts deeper each day, until he quite loses power to see out from them; another, in the same vocation, shows an ability to make each day's work a source of new growth in power. The programme of the first man is much like the squirrel in his revolving cage. He works mighty hard, going through the motions, but is he actually improving his position?

THE "BRITISH ASSOCIATION OF DISPLAY MEN"

has been formed with the object of bringing ALL DISPLAY MEN together (*all trades*) to help one another, exchange ideas for the best results, to make the

"BRITISH DISPLAY MAN" the leading Window Artist of the WORLD

Fill up the Membership Form opposite and post to the Secretary at once:

F. STAPLEY,
The British Association of Display Men,
28, PORTUGAL STREET, LONDON, W.C.2.

'The British Association of Display Men' advertisement featuring in *Display* in the early 1920s.

105

continued to have had a rather erratic existence. In 1939 the editor of *Display* was still bemoaning:

> … to-day there are many first-class men who are working under the most difficult circumstances in situations where the outlook of their employers is completely out of sympathy with their own enthusiastic aspirations.

And even after WWII the status of display personnel was not much stronger. In 1947 their then President, Sir Charles Tennyson, addressed store owners directly:

> To the management of our large stores I would say, engage a really live display manager, if you have not already done so, pay him well and give him a free hand. The policy behind the window is your concern; the expression of that policy is what you are paying him for. If it is worthwhile employing a specialist it is worthwhile giving him authority in his own sphere. Too many shopkeepers are keeping a dog and barking themselves.

The other side of the display personnel picture was provided by an out-of-town store director, Helen Gibson of W. Rowntree & Sons Ltd., who had previously been, herself, a remarkable display woman:

> Display people are business men and women not artists … sometimes they like to be temperamental, and so appear unstable; and yet they are surprised when the management does not give them the important position in the firm they feel they deserve. Display people should impress that they are business-like and are out to sell rather than trying to make the place look pretty. Display is only 50% art.

Nevertheless the post-war professional body began to strengthen, and in 1951, following the route of other creative associations, as the Society of Industrial Artists & Designers, it started to offer Fellowships to acknowledge outstanding contributors to display, the first batch including Eric Lucking of Liberty's. An allied issue contributing to display's inferiority complex was the limited

Above
The Reimann School, Regency Street, Westminster, *Display*, 1937.

Above right
Lettering Class, Reimann School, *Commercial Art*, 1939.

provision for, and recognition of its knowledge and skill in national educational and training schemes. As with professionalism, *Display* was intermittently arguing for effective college courses as in an editorial of 1927:

> Display is getting beyond the stage when a man with ordinary inclinations can dress a window that will 'answer the purpose', It is becoming a highly skilled matter and as it develops so will it get further beyond the capabilities of the uninstructed person ... The time will come when display will figure in the syllabus of every Arts and Crafts school ...

But courses relating to window display remained patchy across the country and, where they did exist, were usually short or part-time evening ones. In London, over the period covered by this book, a number of colleges are noted as offering some sort of relevant training, at one time or another, including Goldsmiths' College, Borough Polytechnic, Sir John Cass, Central School,

Westminster School of Art, Regent Street Polytechnic, and then, with an altogether greater assurance, the College of Distribution [variously titled].

In the inter-war years a number of private schools opened in London specifically for display training including one run by Edward Goldsman, who had been in charge of Selfridges display. But the whole concept of display education was turned upside down with the arrival in London in 1936 of the Reimann School from Berlin. The related press, including *Commercial Art* and *Art & Industry*, had already carried glowing accounts of this wonder school which had started up in 1902 and, by the early 1920s, was offering 'window display' as a main subject. It relocated itself to London, with the threatening rise of National Socialism in Germany, and settled into an impressive building in Victoria. Cleverly it set up an advisory committee consisting of such British luminaries as Jack Beddington of Shell and McKnight Kauffer, the celebrated poster designer; and had on its teaching staff the likes of Milner Gray, with Austin Cooper as Principal. Frank Pick of London Transport attending a Reimann School students' exhibition urged practitioners to visit:

> … it will give you a dreadful shock and will reduce all your window dressing to rubbish when you see it.

For a brief period, prior to WWII, the influence of the Reimann School publicised the practice of display to a professionalism the public and, indeed the store entrepreneurs, perhaps, had not previously appreciated. But with the onset of war the School was forced to close and the professionalization of display was on hold for the next five years.

In spite of all this, a number of individuals, through their talents, energy and personality distinguished themselves in London store publicity and display during this period, some to actually gain directorships in the stores they served. Most of these people are now entirely forgotten or only remembered, if at all, by a small handful of researchers in the history of retailing. Here are a few who definitely deserve a better legacy.

William Crawford was a larger than life personality, who dominated the advertising world in the inter-war years. There were few committees relating to advertising and publicity, and sometimes even art and design, that he didn't serve on, in some capacity or other. He was knighted in 1927 for his publicity work for the Empire Marketing Board, he was publicity advisor to the Ministry of Agriculture in 1929 and the Chairman of the Publicity Committee for the Post Office in the 1930s.

Yet he was a late starter in his career. Not being particularly scholarly he left school early and joined a Scottish opticians, Lazaar, working for them in Liverpool. It is not clear why, in 1906, he left Liverpool and the opticians' world, and came to London to work as a space canvasser, but it is said that he had heard that advertising was the thing of the future and he had decided to be part of it.

He joined the agency F.E. Potter, where he was described as 'energetic and full of fire'. There he wrote his own copy and even worked out his own designs in collaboration with the Carlton Studios. It was only in 1914, when he was thirty-six, that he decided it was time to set up his own agency, which he did in two rooms in Kingsway. Holding fire during WWI, he really got established immediately after the war, when he moved to 233 High Holborn, which was to be Crawford's Head Office during his lifetime.

By 1928 *Commercial Art* was hyping his work enthusiastically:

> For advertising to have its Scotch leader in accordance with the fitness of things long established in our Anglo-Saxon polity …

Crawford's qualities, that were to bring him success and honours, are given by his biographer Saxon Mills:

> The sudden flash of the shrewd idea; the inspiration gathered from a few

Sir William Crawford, founder of Crawford's Advertising Agency.

Celebrities of Advertising
III.—SIR WILLIAM S. CRAWFORD, K.B.E.
Drawing by " bil "

minutes thought and translated on to the scale of big business; the flair; his insight into human nature.

He was to work with a number of London stores including Jaeger and Liberty's, but his major long-standing client was to be Simpson's of Piccadilly. Simpsons had started as a clothing manufacturer in the East End of London aiming to make ready-to-wear clothes as respectable as bespoke. There they had showrooms where retailers could come to see the new ranges and buy.

In 1932 the founder, Simeon Simpson, died, and his son, Alexander [Alec], aged only thirty, became the firm's managing director. Alec was a great sportsman, and the story goes that he disliked wearing braces when he was playing golf and this led to the braceless trousers – DAKS. It was at this point of time that William Crawford was brought in to launch the DAKS campaign.

By 1936, when Alec opened his 'modernist' store in Piccadilly, Crawford had become something of a father figure to him. Crawford, with his exceptional designer, Ashley Havinden, and his illustrator, Max Hoff, could be said to have developed one of the earliest corporate identity schemes for Simpson's. Havinden's work for the store is rated not only one of the most long-lasting integrated design schemes, but one of the most distinguished. Crawford held the agency for Simpson's through to his death in 1950, and, what must have been very rare for an advertising man, became a director of the company, and so could actually influence its policies rather than merely illustrate them.

An overlapping campaign run by Crawford was for Jaeger, which, in the 1930s was making tentative steps towards modernism. Crawford took over the Jaeger account in 1930 and made a major contribution to its regeneration as an up-to-date company, no longer tied to its healthy woolly past. Antonia White, the writer, who was working as a copywriter at the time, described in *Commercial Art* Crawford's campaign for Jaeger as having 'modern spirits'; as

110

dynamic and dashing with a quality of 'gay improvisation'. She wrote of the
Crawford copy:

> exaggerated, willful, even exasperating, made a complete break with
> traditional 'fashion-copy', and instanced old ladies as threatening to close
> their accounts and agents shaking their heads.

Crawford's work for Liberty began in 1947, only some three years before
his death. Liberty's was not only coping with the post-war challenges for
redevelopment being experienced across the board by London stores, but was
coming to realise that their pre-war 'arts and crafts' reputation was by then
'out-of-fashion'. Crawford's was asked to design a corporate image, as they had
done for Simpson's in the '30s. Ashley Havinden's starry 'L' became Liberty's
'house-mark', appearing not only in press advertising but on all their packaging
and display material and literature.

Crawford, beside his advertising work for stores, did much to further the
cause of display, and to strengthen the link between display and advertising.
He was the advertising man most frequently mentioned in *Display* columns;
spent time lecturing along the lines that display should be a high ranking
branch of selling; and was to feature at many professional events – his first of a
number of talks being to the British Association of Display Men in 1926.

Crawford had the energy and focus of a pioneer opening up the west, the
imagination of a visionary, and the persuasiveness of an evangelist; 'un home
excessif', he brought modernism to London store advertising.

Edward N. Goldsman, the doyen of display men

When Gordon Selfridge declared that a good displayman should be paid well for his professionalism, he was asked where such a paragon could be found; he stated baldly – 'America'. So when, in 1908, he founded Selfridges & Co. Ltd. in Oxford Street, true to his word, he looked to America, bringing over Edward Goldsman to run his display department. Goldsman was not only paid well, but reported directly to the Board, a status which must have been unique for a displayman at that time.

Gordon Honeycombe, in his history of Selfridges, refers to Goldsman as a 'senior employee brought over from America' with the assumption that he was 'pinched' from Marshall Fields. However, a reference in *Display* describes Goldsman as resigning his post as principal of a correspondence school in order to join Selfridge in London, and, given his subsequent career, this may well be the more reliable account.

Goldsman's rather refined appearance [he is said to have looked like a lawyer or a literary man], and quiet voice, belied the dynamism within that was not only to make Selfridges the leading store when it came to display, but enabled Goldsman to dominate the British retail display scene between the wars.

Goldsman was something of an intellectual, a rarity among display professionals. He linked what was going on, on the drawing board and in the workshop of a store display department, not only with the obvious – the economy of the country – but liked to trace such activities back to the processions of the Ridings in the 13th century, and was also wont to encourage his fellow professionals to source their ideas for displays from contemporary art movements. His giving display an historical context, and associating it with fine art, endowed it with a dignity and status that would have been incomprehensible to most window trimmers of the 1910s. To so many of these, who crammed their windows with merchandise, a description of how Goldsman went about his work could well have seemed bizarre:

Edward N. Goldsman [on left] at an international display conference, 1920.

> Every idea, scheme or design after submission to the head of the business [in Goldsman's case Gordon Selfridge], has to be carefully studied before a working design and plans can be produced. This necessitates research work at museums and libraries, visits at times to centres of manufacture, and also, occasionally, to historical locations.

Although many of the ideas for Selfridges' displays and publicity came from Selfridge himself, certainly the more 'stunt' ones, it was Goldsman who brought in the concept of design, the aesthetic element. It was Goldsman who claimed to have introduced 'open dressing' to England, the thinning down of merchandise in the window and its artistic grouping. He frequently declared the essence of good display to be simplicity, workmanship, neatness, and inexpensiveness. His motto – 'what was good enough for my father is not good enough for me', stressed his progressive stance.

Goldsman urged what he must have considered his 'backwood' colleagues not only to look to America for examples of adventurous display, but also to look to the rumblings from the Continent – 'the careless vivacity and grace' of the French, and the 'solidity and strength' of the Germans. He introduced British display to the geometric forms of the Cubists, to the abstraction of the Futurists, and, most enthusiastically, to the work of a fellow American who came to live in London – McKnight Kauffer [who was to have as great an influence on British poster design as Goldsman was to have on display].

Goldsman recommended his display brethren to open their eyes and minds to such modernistic styles as those of McKnight Kauffer's, which he sold as 'arresting, attracting attention, carrying power and having memorability'. His plea was for display men to 'break away from their present banalities'. Of his many designs for Selfridges' displays, perhaps Goldsman's most striking were for the 1911 Coronation of George V and Queen Mary, for Selfridges 10th anniversary in 1919, and for the signing of the Peace Treaty in the same year. It was typical of him that when he decided to use heraldic devices for the

Coronation, he had the Royal College of Heralds check for the accuracy of his design. He ran a crimson valance round the building, embroidered with the King's monogram and had 12 feet high shields, bearing the arms of previous kings, with over 4,500 bulbs used to light the shields; nothing quite like it had been seen before in the West End.

Not only did Goldsman shake up the design of London store display, but he did much to raise the status of display men. In the States he had been a past-President of the International Association of Window Trimmers and, in London, he was to become the first President of the British Association of Display Men. He was to spend some time travelling around the country with a lantern slide 'showing off' good examples of display work and drumming up enthusiasm for the Association. He was oftimes scathing of the situation as he found it:

> I sometimes marvel how some [display managers] hold their jobs. I can only
> imagine that the business itself, the manager and the buyers, are all of the
> stiff conservative outlook, and we can't hope for better things until they are
> all pensioned off.

In 1920 he retired from the Association on the grounds of ill-health, and he left Selfridges in 1924. But that was by no means the last that was heard of him. He went on to write numerous articles on display, including a chapter 'An historical survey of British Window Display' in H. Ashford Davis's *The Art of Window Display*. And he started his own school of display, which appears to have gone through several metamorphoses for by 1934 it was named the New Goldsman School of Window Display and by 1939 it had become Goldsman's Correspondence College – 'learn modern window display at home'. Presumably with aging, he no longer had the energy to run a school but could work in a more sedentary way from his home, from which he also seems to have run a book business, selling new and second-hand books on his subject.

His letter of congratulations to the journal *Display* on its 21st birthday in 1940, when he was poignantly described as 'very ill' encapsulates his life as a displayman:

> At night when I am unable to sleep I go over in my mind all the lectures, all the judging of competitions, all the meetings, and I think of all the big towns in England where I have attended in the interest of display. All the people I have met rise up in my mind and I think with gratitude of the respect and courtesy with which they have received me and my message. I think of the hundreds and hundreds of young men and women I have tried my best to train and of the long list of display friends I have in many countries of the world. Then my mind switches on to the great exhibitions I have taken part in, and so I join with the rest of the self-respecting British display interests in sending greetings to *Display* on its 21st birthday.

Leon Goodman, Display Supplier

From the 1930s, through the war and into the early post-war years, Leon Goodman was a dominant figure in store display, being one of the major suppliers. His influence lay not only in his being at the forefront of the development of shop fittings, but in his own personal conviction that display was not a marginal activity, and he, as supplier, merely marginal to it. He saw display as central to the whole image of a store, part and parcel of its publicity and advertising in building that image – he was a major player in 'putting display on the map'.

Goodman was an aspiring young man who, from some basic art training, had taken his portfolio of advertising ideas round the agencies in London, demanding that he be immediately allowed to devise some colossal campaign for them. Frustrated in his ambitions by their reluctance to take him on board,

115

Announcing!

The **NEW**

GOLDSMAN SCHOOL
of WINDOW DISPLAY

(Licensed by the L.C.C.)

-
-
-

UNDER THE DIRECTION of
MR. E. N. GOLDSMAN
AND   Ex-President I.A.D.M.
MR. JOHN HUNT, A.R.C.A.

**DESIGN • COLOUR • COMPOSITION
MODERN ARCHITECTURE • LIGHTING
LETTERING • FIGURE DRAPING • INTERIOR
AND EXTERIOR STORE DECORATION
STAFF TRAINING • COSTUME DRAWING
FROM LIFE • AIR BRUSH TECHNIQUE, ETC.**

THE ONLY SCHOOL OF ITS
KIND TEACHING THE PRACTICAL
APPLICATION OF MODERN DISPLAY
METHODS FOR COMMERCIAL AND
INDUSTRIAL PURPOSES . . . .

4, GROTTO PASSAGE, PADDINGTON STREET
Tel: Welbeck 5883   **BAKER STREET, W.1**

Advertisement for Goldsman's School of Window Display, 1934–5.

Advertisement for Leon Goodman Displays Ltd., 1937.

he turned to display supplies for a career, determining to champion display as an advertising adjunct.

Advertisements for Leon Goodman Displays Ltd. began to appear in the late 1930s. From the start the reader was made aware that this was no small house selling floral decorations or wax mannequins. The name, 'Leon Goodman Displays Ltd.' was always accompanied by the slogan 'The House of Ideas', which he also had emblazoned across the front of his warehouse. Here was no jobbing carpenter or a manufacturer of novelties but an intellectual, no subordinate sub-serving the display directors of the stores but someone who could, at the very least, be additive, and, more likely, spear-heading and progressive, leading the way.

Leon Goodman started his shopfitting supply business in Finsbury Park, but by July 1937 had moved it to the West End, to Whitfield Street, behind Oxford Street and Tottenham Court Road, from where it offered a complete display service for 'buildings, streets, windows and interiors'. His press advertising was impressive both in size, in the use of humour, [a rarity with display suppliers], and in the overwhelming self-confidence it exuded. It addressed the reader personally, with much use of the word 'we'. A typical example of Goodman's style was one of his press advertisements that solely consisted of text, no image:

> Sorry, what's the use! We have catalogued over two hundred superb display items of all kinds and we just couldn't make up our minds as to the best one to illustrate here.

Goodman, himself, was a considerable self-publicist, appearing in print in the display press with articles and letters on any, and every, aspect of display; and popping up in numerous news items – as speaker here and there, as extending his business interests this way and that, and even getting himself a broadcasting spot speaking to America about wartime conditions in England, and a film slot in a March of Time film on preparations for the Coronation.

By the late '40s Goodman had acquired a number of subsidiaries – Keystudios providing large scenery painted canvases [including some for Covent Garden]; Pageantry Ltd. which supplied appropriately garbed personnel for banquets or events and the ilk; Ace Publicity providing displays linked to the theatre and to films; along with his company's London Exhibition Centre for out-of-town firms to display their wares in the Capital; his imagination, energy and enterprise knew no bounds.

Much of Goodman's public speaking was on behalf of his professional body – the Association of Display Producers and Silk Screen Printers, of which he was President. The image he sought for his industry he described as:

> Not the pompous parade of side and swagger … nor yet the circus parade of
> flamboyance, frippery and flounce … of great promise but little substance …
> but, rather, a rational parade of reasoned presentation in fact a 'Show-off',
> but sincere and with a purpose.

This statement was in a booklet he produced in 1938 – 'Parade for Profit'
which was a collation of what sixty-four key personalities of the time thought
about display. By gathering together the words of the great and the good in
one volume, Goodman presumably hoped to gain status by association, for
amongst his 'personalities' were not only the editors of *Advertising Monthly* and
Advertising Weekly, but William Crawford of the leading advertising agency of
the time, and Misha Black, the exhibition designer.

Goodman actually had the confidence to take on the advertising agencies,
speaking at a number of their conferences and dinners, pleading the role
of display:

> Let it be clear that we do not challenge all other advertising media and
> complacently suggest that we can replace them … we are about showing the
> product, and showing it at the point where the public is most likely to buy.

In fact Goodman did, occasionally, give the impression that he actually did
consider 'display' the superior element in any campaign, compared to 'trumpet-
tongue media screeching questionable claims'.

His leadership was particularly to the fore in wartime when he wrote and
spoke along the lines 'down with pessimism and defeatism and misguided
economies', and urged his colleagues to a 'constructive optimism'; that wartime
restrictions provided opportunities for invention. He, himself, with rationing
of paper and print, experimented with posters on woven fabrics, and exploited
the necessity of boarded store windows by decorating the hoardings, including
displays to cover the sandbags! He managed, like many of the stores, to use
patriotism to his advantage.

As a mere 'supplier' Goodman could be said to have operated at a level unusual to his industry, but thereby he not only raised its status, but that of 'display' generally, having the chutzpah to equate his contribution to those of the advertising agencies and publicists.

Edward Grieve of Harrods

Edward William Grieve was one of the longest serving display men of London stores. He joined Harrods in 1924 at the age of 18. Although he doesn't seem to have settled, leaving in 1926, he appears to have returned a year later and, from then onwards was to work loyally through to 1953 being appointed senior displayman when the previous holder left.

Grieve had wanted to work in display from his boyhood, when he had been fascinated by the way goods were displayed in the shop windows of his home town, Kirkliston, in Scotland. On leaving school he joined a large store in Edinburgh on the merchandising side but soon got himself moved into display.

Although Grieve was ambitious he seems to have had a very different personality to that of Goldsman, the displayman who had set the trend at Selfridges, Harrods great rivals. Grieve comes across as a modest, moderate man, well able to compromise when necessary. He was not to be found on the lecture circuit, wrote little about his work, and was not caught up in professional politics. If he was featured in the display press, which he frequently was, it was largely with images of his work, briefly captioned to point out the originality of his designs. Yet, in spite of his disinclination to 'show off', in 1938, *Art and Industry* chose to feature him as the representative of British display to be compared with Tom Lee of Bonwit Teller, New York, declaring that:

Grieve's wartime window at Harrods,
December 1940.

Edward Grieve ... compelled attention from both the trade and public, and probably in London there is to-day no other store within striking distance of Harrods' brilliant windows.

And it was Grieve, by his steady contributions, presented without fanfares, who received the unique accolade, for display personnel, of being made Royal Designer of Industry in 1940. He is the only display person to have become an RDI. [Natasha Kroll who was also to become an RDI was recognized more for her work in television than in store display].

Yet curiously, Grieve reported that he was unable to draw, and that none of his ideas were worked out on paper. He would visualize a window and then describe his ideas to his staff, who would translate them into swathes and drapes – whatever. His mind was forever on the job, whether he was on holiday or even sitting reading. He said he could never get through a book as practically everything he read would trigger off a display possibility.

Although when asked about his work he was wont to speak in general impersonal terms, nevertheless this could oftimes reveal something about his own approach to his work as in this rare reported talk entitled 'Display Sense':

> ... a display man is born, not made; he is gifted with the vision of an inward eye and is able to visualize a finished picture when shown the merchandise in the merchant's hand.

And ...

> He [the diplay man] must not run away with the idea that he is something better than man, put on earth to live on a plane of his own, surrounded by slaves who at the clap of his hands will run to do his bidding.

Grieve was particularly aware of the sensitivity of the displayman – buyer relationship. He recommended his colleagues to carry a notebook with them, and to make use of it, whoever they were listening to, ever aware of the ideas and

121

Grieve on his honeymoon cruise, 1951.

concerns of whoever was talking, and that would have included the buyer and other co-workers as well as the customer. He actually used the word 'popular', to stress the need of display people to be 'liked', as they were so dependent on the co-operation of others. Grieve himself seems to have been immensely popular, certainly with Harrods staff, acting, at times, as the President of the Staff Entertainment Society. Grieve was not only concerned about the buyer – displayman relationship but with how display could work in with the company's advertising and publicity. He saw display as the twin ally of advertising:

> Advertising in newspapers … should also be closely followed by the display man, and he should endeavor to get an actual presentation of the advertised image in the window and in the department where the merchandise is sold.

Grieve was essentially a company man and his long stay at Harrods could be related not only to the distinction of his work but to his ability to fit in. He understood how to work in with buyers, department heads and publicity staff, and could subsume his own ambitions and ideas to those of the organization:

> You must first learn from the Directors of the House what the policy of the store actually is, and then not merely follow it out because you are asked to do so, but live it, become absorbed in it, make it you – you it.

His total devotion to duty is exemplified by an incident in 1936, when he was on holiday on the Continent and received a telephone call to his hotel announcing the death of the King. He caught the first available plane home, early the next day, a Tuesday, and by Wednesday the whole of Harrods' windows, numbering in all nearly a hundred, were changed to mourning.

As far as his actual display work was concerned, Grieve was particularly noted for his use of colour:

> The importance of colour in window display cannot be too strongly stressed. It makes the spectator gay, and if she is gay she wants to spend.

He was one of the first to spray the mannequins whatever colour would work in with the particular display in mind and managed to achieve a remarkable white porcelain finish when they were used for Harrods' 'White Sales'. Grieve was particularly fond of dark blue, not only for the bases supporting the mannequins but for backgrounds, declaring blue 'blacker than black'. An especially notorious display of his had models with sprayed pale pink legs, sky blue shoes, and deep Oriental blue bases. *Display* recommending it to out-of-town display men wrote of it – 'If you want to cause a sensation in your home town try it sometime'.

One of many triumphs for Grieve was his remarkable display for the visit of the French President to London in 1939. He chose to have the forty windows dressed entirely in white, the windows framed in muslin, and the merchandise backed by enormous white fans, made up of wood, lace and organdie. The mannequins all sported French, or French derived clothes and were accompanied by prancing French poodles and 2,000 fleurs-de-lys.

Without aiming for sensation Grieve, well aware of trends in display at home and internationally, took what he felt he could use from technical and aesthetic developments. As early as 1938 he was experimenting with Perspex with one of his most striking displays where the heads of his mannequins were separated, and suspended above their bodies.

Wartime conditions brought to the fore the total focused practicality of Grieve. He immediately appreciated the effect of the restraints on display of government rationing and scarcity of supplies but decided this was not to frustrate him but actually to challenge his creativity, and this conclusion he sold to his professional colleagues in a rare article in *Display*:

> War may cancel all contracts, alter all plans, change one's habits, but its one redeeming factor is perhaps to reveal the skill of the display man. Many men can achieve clever results by commissioning artists and designers baited with a fat cheque, but in wartime a slenderer cheque, or perhaps none at all, calls

for ingenuity, and the display man who is ordinarily extravagantly inclined rather revels in the achievement of keeping up his standard at a self-inflicted deflated budget.

Grieve's wartime windows moved quickly from lace and picture frames to wheelbarrows and rakes. One display that was well received was entitled 'leaflet raid' and had a model aircraft supposedly dropping leaflets on the enemy – the leaflets being pages from Harrods catalogues. Another noteworthy and courageous of Grieve's wartime windows showed Doris Zinkeisen's drawings of civilians injured in the air-raids, on behalf of the Duke of Gloucester's Red Cross and St. John's Fund. *Display* said of his work – 'Harrods have kept up a wonderful standard of work for wartime and with a much depleted and young staff'.

Grieve's unself-trumpeted worthiness as a displayman was acknowledged not only by his displays continuing to be considered newsworthy, but by his being elected an RDI. In 1951, at the age of forty-nine, to the surprise of his colleagues who had seen him as 'married to his work', Grieve married a diplomat's daughter, Madame de la Torre, who was, at the time, employed by Harrods to boost its overseas trading. It was presumably this happy event that triggered his retirement from Harrods soon afterwards!

Martha Harris, Display Consultant

Martha Harris, an American, 'hit' the London store display scene in the late 1920s and shone brightly for some half a dozen years, disappearing with the suddenness of her arrival. She had been educated at Harvard and, intent on some sort of literary career, had come to London. At first she worked on a women's paper and then for a publisher, moving to their publicity side. This interested her first in posters, and then in what she termed 'three-dimensional

Martha Harris, the only woman at a display dinner, 1937.

posters', the shop window. She described her display career as starting around 1925 in New York when she dressed a bookshop window. From this she seems to have drifted into actual store display becoming interior display manager for a New York department store – an indication, perhaps, of her forceful, confident character, as she had had no formal design training and had very little relevant experience to offer.

Returning to England, her first commission, in 1928, was for Jaeger. It is possible that this came via Crawford's advertising agency as she is known to have obtained her clients initially via this route and she considered them the most 'modern' and therefore most suited to her intent. Her description of this first display assignment, not only tells of the origins of her style of 'flat' dressing, but also of her attitudes to display, to the people who worked in it, and reveals something of her personality:

> I spent the week-end working day and night in an intensive effort to learn the art of window-dressing in forty-eight hours without any instruction. Not being hampered with any training whatever in this direction I simply analysed the situation and selected the merchandise to go into the window

entirely on the basis of its attractiveness and colour consistency. Then I began folding it into shapes that suited the design of the window. That was the beginning of the new type of 'flat dressing' which marked the revolution in window dressing at Jaeger shops. The selling value of this type of dressing as against the usual method of draping on T-stands or portly busts was immediately apparent, and five guinea jumpers and expensive suits simply walked out of the windows into the possession of interested customers.

This extract shows that Harris could be totally hands-on when this was required although she saw herself primarily as a designer and not a dresser. In her early days in London she was to complain incessantly of the workmen and their

PERDITA
Papier Mache display figure in full round, cream colour. Arms and hands detachable

Price £8 : 10 : 0
free delivery London

Martha

New Ideas for Windows

New Studios. New Factory. Bigger and better facilities for design and construction. Single windows — or national display campaigns. Consult us if you are in search of new ideas.

MARTHA HARRIS, Ltd., 119 Copenhagen Street, London, N. 1.   Telephone : Terminus 4957

Harris Ltd

Advertisement for Martha Harris in *Display*, 1935.

127

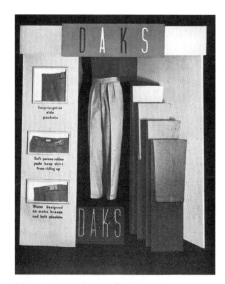

Martha Harris display for Daks
trousers, 1935.

inadequate execution of her ideas, protesting that first-rate design [hers!] could so frequently be ruined by fifth-rate execution and advising display designers to trust no-one at any stage.

> I have learnt all the techniques of woodwork and construction through
> having to cope with the incompetencies of carpenters for so many years.

All this suggests that Martha Harris was something of a hard taskmaster, a stickler for standards – 'no wrinkles, puckers or gaps' – and generally a controller rather than an enabler. She herself admitted that the people who worked for her had a real 'fear' of her detecting their mistakes.

Although she introduced the idea of 'flat' dressing [merely laying the garments flat or leaning them against a prop], and was extremely imaginative in her displays, Martha Harris despised what she described as 'the flighty arty type of person', coming into the profession from art school, considering display work to be '95% practical knowledge and commercial experience and 5% artistic sense'; in this she seems to be taking her own career as the sole model for advancement.

Martha Harris appears to have worked mainly in a freelance capacity from the start. Her need to control all aspects of her work and her perfectionist standards fairly quickly led her to appreciate that she would only be satisfied if she ran her own show. By 1934 she was advertising her own consultancy, offering near-total display services including overall design, actual window settings, along with display figures. An early advertisement suggests an impatience to launch herself for the blurb concludes with the unfinished sentence 'A number of these figures, ideas and designs are ready now …' suggesting that some were not and that she had rather got ahead of herself. Nevertheless there was an openness, a 'tell it as it is' style to her self-advertisement for she was one of the rare display consultancies to declare her rates in her publicity.

Her considerable self-confidence and originality seem to have been a combination for success, for by 1934 she had moved her operation from her home in Hampstead to a studio in Marylebone High Street and, by the next year to new studios and a factory in Copenhagen Street. Her commission for a DAKS display unit for Simpson's went national; these were identical units sent out to retailers all over the country who were agents for DAKS and the success of these must have helped fill the coffers. Her reputation would have been also

Martha Harris display for Jaeger, 1935.

furthered by Martha Harris Ltd. supervising, on behalf of Jaeger, one of the nine windows in the Display Exhibition put on at Burlington House.

By 1937 Martha Harris was regularly appearing in publicity photos – giving advice for an overseas exhibition alongside a government minister, or next to a distinguished American overseas displayman at a dinner in his honour – Arthur V. Fraser from Marshall Fields; it was a rarity to see any woman present on such display occasions.

Although Martha Harris comes across as a self-centred, determinedly confident woman, a more generous side is shown in an article in *Art & Industry* in 1936 on the illustrator Pearl Falconer, whose drawings she bought and whom she encouraged to design for display. In this Martha Harris is described as able to nurture young talent as well as chastise it:

> Martha Harris, who so successfully develops the latent talent for three-dimensional display that many commercial artists hardly suspect themselves of possessing...

Martha Harris saw herself as a reformer – demanding a higher status for display in the retail world, and, in parallel, demanding higher standards within the display world itself to merit it. Whatever she demanded of others she asked of herself, and she can only attract sympathy and admiration when one reads of the satisfaction she derived from her display work:

> ... when a whopping great window is finished, when the last brawl about the quality of the work has quietened down, when the neighbourhood clocks strike the wee small hours, and you go out into the street to see the result of your work, you get a thrill of satisfaction and pride and boundless enjoyment that few other experiences in life can touch. It is almost as satisfactory as being in love – and who can say more than that.

Natasha Kroll, Simpson's Display Director

In 1967 Ashley Havinden, at the time Deputy Master of the Faculty of Royal Designers for Industry, presented Natasha Kroll, when she was received into the Faculty for her work on Window Display and Television Design, [probably with more emphasis on the latter than the former]. Natasha, and Grieve of Harrods, are the only RDI to date to have 'Window Display' listed as the medium for their election.

Natasha was born in Moscow in 1914, but when she was eight her family moved to Germany and it was there that she received her basic training in window display at the Reimann Schule. It was customary, at the School, to select a number of approved students as paid assistants, and it was in this capacity that she worked, for some four years, when the school relocated to London in 1936.

Her first job as a professional in window display was at the Rowntree's Department Stores, in Scarborough and York. By the 1930s Rowntree's had built up a considerable reputation for adventurous displays and were one of the few stores out of London to have their windows featured regularly in *Display*. In 1942 she returned to London to join Simpson's of Piccadilly. Simpson had not only commissioned the radical architect Joseph Emberton for his new store but had employed the temporary Bauhaus emigree, Moholy-Nagy, to design much of the interiors and windows, and had Ashley Havinden design the store's carpets – Simpson's shone as one of the most modernist of stores. And even when Alec died prematurely and his doctor brother Samuel became deputy chairman the emphasis on modernism was continued, providing Natasha with a sympathetic culture within which she could develop her own brand of European progressiveness.

Natasha was to stay at Simpson's some twelve years, working her way up successfully from Display Manager to taking on the comprehensive responsibility for all the store's design, display and publicity work. She seems to have been given a relatively free rein to exercise her imagination, or 'free' as far as wartime

Natasha Kroll, RDI.

Simpson's display from design by André François.

Book cover of Natasha Kroll's
Window Display, 1954.

conditions allowed. She responded to the challenge by making much use of what nowadays would be described as 'found' objects – barbed wire, string, old ladders, bricks, crates – whatever was at hand. So clever was her ingenuity, that she can be said to have devised a fashionable new style of display that caused some stir in the profession for she was juxtaposing very high quality clothes with rough-edged makeshift materials. Natasha's imagination would also occasionally take a quirky turn [not unlike that of Barbara Jones, her contemporary], one example being her 'imprisoning' a fur coat, apparently tossing a ball, in a large cage on wheels drawn by two other fur coats draped as if pulling reins.

No wartime topic was beyond her idiosyncratic imagination. When clothes rationing was introduced she 'taught' her would-be customers by having a large blackboard in the window on which was spelt out how many coupons were needed for which articles; and, when rationing stopped, she filled the windows with waste paper baskets stuffed with the now redundant clothing coupons.

By 1945 *Display* was reporting:

> Simpson's of Piccadilly is now a household word, thanks to good advertising, and the windows have never once been drab and uninteresting – which says a great deal for Miss Kroll, in charge of displays.

Her chutzpah seemed to know no bounds for she seems to have extended her domain to the outside of the store as well. In 1943 she bedecked its frontage with flags for Merchant Navy Week; and it was Natasha who invented Simpson's great Christmas tree of lights, stretching along the whole Piccadilly frontage – a tradition that was continued even after she left the company.

Natasha became so key to Simpson's operations that when, in 1948, the joint Managing Director, Major Huskisson, planned an American coast-to-coast export drive, Natasha was to accompany him. Together they travelled to New York, Dallas, San Francisco and Los Angeles, meeting with some forty store and display people, including the international renowned Tom Lee at Bergdorf Goodman's. She found much to commend American display and was particularly struck by the fact that how the interiors should look tended to be an integral part of the initial store design and not something added on as an afterthought. Nevertheless she considered the 'largesse of riches' available to the New York stores led to a 'lack of restraint' and was not always in good taste and consequently recommended that:

> … in the men's window by showing few pieces of merchandise with
> perfectly matched accessories, good craftsmanship and good taste, we
> will raise our prestige and give confidence to our potential customer that
> whatever he buys in our Store will be correct and in impeccable taste.

She put on DAKS exhibitions both in New York and Los Angeles virtually single-handed, having something of a challenge recruiting young Hollywood extras to look sufficiently British to show off the clothes.

Her report of the trip contained highly detailed recommendations and it was to serve as a guide to the setting up of the new Simpson's Women's department, as well as forwarding the progress of an Export Department, which was established within two years of the visit, designed by Natasha herself.

Natasha built up a loyal team around her and was ever alert to new talent. From the field of illustration she recruited André François to design a cigar smoking Father Christmas display, menu cards for the restaurant and a set of Simpson's playing cards. And she gave the young Terence Conran, just out of art school, his first display commission. It was Conran who supplied the line drawings for her book 'Window Display' in the Studio 'How to do it' series.

Although Natasha's ideas for Simpson's displays may have alarmed the more traditional of her professional colleagues, when she came to put on paper her thoughts she comes across as eminently sensible and practical [both in her report on the American trip and in her book]; her recommendations are down-to-earth without emotional frills or furbelows or exhortations. In fact any reader of her book, which came out towards the end of her time at Simpson's [in 1954], may well be disappointed at how straightforward, unquirky, merely stating the obvious, it reads. What is very clear is that however artistically imaginative she was, Natasha, at heart, was a merchandiser; she knew her job was about selling. She pointed out in her book that obviously a window should not bore; that its job was to arrest the attention of the passer–by and persuade them to enter the store, but reminds the reader:

> the actual job of selling begins in front of your window, and the part display plays in it is as important as that of the salesman who writes the bill.

Sir Hugh Casson, in the introduction to her book, described Natasha as 'one of the most skilful and imaginative display designers in the country'; and her obituaries, in 2004, were equally laudatory. Although much of what was written about her related to her work at the BBC, which she joined soon after leaving Simpson's, and where she carved out a most distinguished career pioneering production design for television, her work in display was not forgotten. The *Observer's* tribute by Bernard Lodge was typical:

> To both strands of her career she brought a creative sensibility that was rooted in the progressive design philosophy of pre-war Europe, and, like many of her fellow Europeans who settled in Britain in the 1930s, she enriched the visual language of her adopted country.

Eric Lucking of Liberty's

> London had its own genius in Eric Lucking whose dressing of Liberty's windows was so outstanding that, as an art-struck schoolboy, I used to voyage just to stand and stare in wonder at them.
> – Roy Strong, *The Times*, 1984

Eric Lucking, who was to become Liberty's Publicity and Display Manager in 1945, was a displayman through and through. Before joining Liberty's he had

Liberty's window display by Eric Lucking, advertising the Young Liberty boutique, opened in 1949.

served a lengthy 'apprenticeship', working his way up through the ranks, in a variety of retail outlets, before getting one of the plum jobs, responsible for across the board 'showing off' at the Regent Street store.

His career started at the Army & Navy Store where he worked for some nine and a half years. Later he recalled that it was about this time he actually applied to Liberty's but was found wanting and rejected. It is probable that he had begun to realize that if he wanted to progress he might have to move around, and over the next seven years he worked at D.H. Evans, at the Rivoli Gift Shop in Knightsbridge [where the German owner gave him the opportunity to spend some time in Germany], and at Druce's in Baker Street where he helped with a reorganization for ten months before being called up into the Forces at the beginning of WWII [display not being a protected occupation!].

Lucking was a displayman who put his merchandise first, fully appreciating the role display played in any company's profitability. In *Store* magazine [March 1951], under the title 'to Stardom from Storedom' – a planned series of articles on key retail personnel, Lucking being chosen to start the series – his attitude to display work was baldly stated:

> displayman [not display artist, please, this is one of the terms Mr. Lucking abominates for to him display is a technique of sales promotion, not an 'airy-fairy' art].

It is clear that Lucking had little patience with what he might have called the lunatic fringe of his profession and what he did describe as 'tortured ingenuity' – the artist-displayman who, fitting the goods to his or her design, had no real feeling for merchandise or, for that matter, the company's balance sheet. He once described such pre-war offerings as 'too much gilding of the lily'. Lucking, by getting his inspiration from the objects to be shown, in fact proved to be one of the most artistic of display personnel in the post-WWII years.

It had been the Editor of *Display* who had introduced Lucking to Arthur Stewart Liberty, who then persuaded his Directors to appoint Lucking as their first Display Manager, to create a 'new look' for Liberty's. It was a difficult time to take up such a challenge for government wartime regulations and rationing were still in place and supplies scarce. Alison Adburgham, in her history of Liberty's gives examples of his ingenuity in the face of the austerity of the late '40s and early '50s – making use of any material he could lay his hands on – bits of wood from the bomb sites of Soho for stands, wire and straw for mannequins and blackout curtains stretched and painted white for screens. This last lightened the dull walnut panelling, backing the window space, that was part of his inheritance there, and proved particularly effective as the Ministry of Works was still restricting the amount of artificial light stores could use.

137

Contemporary art in Liberty's window.

Even Sir Richard Burbidge of Harrods wrote to Lucking to tell him that he had made a special journey to Regent Street to see the resulting windows, which he described as 'absolutely enthralling'.

This was praise enough, but probably the reactions of his professional peers was, for Lucking, a better validation of his skill. Natasha Kroll, who was distinguishing herself at Simpsons at the time, included examples of Lucking's work in her book on window display, in which all of her other illustrations were either from Simpson's or from abroad. She seems to have

Example of Lucking's material draping.

been particularly admiring of his 'supreme craftsmanship' in draping, with an example of a mannequin in what appears to be an evening dress but is actually a swathe of material without a pin in it.

And Ashley Havinden, one of the most outstanding designers of store advertising, who had worked with Liberty's, wrote of Lucking in the *Penrose Annual* of 1951:

> The brilliant work of Eric Lucking, who was engaged as display manager,
> soon resulted in Liberty's windows being regarded as outstanding examples
> of contemporary display.

But Lucking was not just a self-absorbed displayman, producing windows after windows to be admired in the press and by all and sundry. He, unselfishly, over the years became an evangelist for raising the status of his profession. Within Liberty's itself he had achieved a position in the managerial chain rarely to be found by display personnel in other stores. Until he arrived each department had been assigned window space, which would be dressed by the departmental buyer and sales staff. It was Lucking who broke this departmental hold and introduced composite cross-departmental windows with the displayman very much in charge. It was not only a matter of who should hold the responsibility for display, but that by display personnel asserting their specialist professionalism actual standards of both display and buying itself could be raised. He wrote of how he found the general status of display professionals:

> Unfortunately the grudging reception and inadequate remuneration meted
> out to the display-minded has deterred many from pursuing the profession.
> It is hardly surprising that few have emerged as prominent executives
> capable of exerting their own personalities to hold in check the many cross
> current which hinder the interests of sound display.

But Lucking had exerted his personality, for not only did he hold the reins of all display work at Liberty's, but he had seen the importance of expressing the

139

store's corporate identity as over-riding departmental interests. And, by taking responsibility for advertising and publicity as well as display, he was able to present a unified face – advertising might get them to the store, but display would get them in.

> If windows were paid for as one would buy advertising space in the press, their market value would rocket to prodigious proportions and the poor relation among the publicity media would not be relegated to obscurity at the first hint of depression.

He worked particularly well with Crawford, whose advertising agency Liberty's was using at the time, frequently being additive to the publicity material being designed.

Lucking is said to have looked, and to have had the manner of, an actor. He certainly had a considerable skill with words, a rarity among display personnel who, judged from the general run of articles in design and display magazines and press such as *Store*, *Display* and *Commercial Art* [later *Art & Industry*], had a tendency to platitudes. He used his verbal fluency to write and speak frequently in order to raise the status of display, oftimes cajoling even store entrepreneurs:

> Those who control the destinies of our stores, if they are indeed conscious of the force which lies at their hands [display], are far too timid or cheese-paring to launch whole-heartedly into its use.

And beyond Liberty's Lucking worked tirelessly for his profession, both in his writing and speechifying. Within the British Display Association he served on committees before becoming its Vice-Chairman in 1950 and Chairman and Fellow in 1951. He raised the status of display in the country both by the example of his own remarkable creative output that led the public to flock to Liberty's at each change of window, and by his proselytizing through his professional body. *Fortune*, the global business magazine, acknowledged Lucking's contribution beyond the London store scene:

E.E. Lucking, a leading light in the modern display world, makes each window a unified composition of form and colour, symbolic, sophisticated, classically simple or dreamily fantastic, sometimes bizarre and surrealist, but always original and imparting to the West End something of the inventive chic belonging to the smartest continental houses.

In spite of all his many activities Lucking appears to have had some time to spare, and, presumably, some freedom as to how he operated, for whilst he was still at Liberty's he seems to have carried out some consultancy work, as that for Misha Black for the Festival of Britain. Such experience would have stood him in good stead when he decided, at the age of fifty, to leave the store in 1956 to set himself up as an independent consultant. He was to have as distinguished a career as such as he had had at Liberty's, working not only with retail companies but with the very manufacturers which had supplied the materials that he had originally 'trimmed' so well himself.

William Roberts poster for the
Sitwell's groundbreaking exhibition
of French Art, 1919.

Appendix I:
'Showing Off' at the Mansard Gallery, Heals

I had intended to write a piece about Lady Gladys Prudence Maufe, as one of London stores' 'show off' personalities, but found insufficient data to present her as a rounded personality. Heal's archive, lodged at the Victoria & Albert Museum contains no mention of her, albeit a photo of her with her husband and two others has the three men named, but no name for her! At least Susanna Gooden in her history of Heals makes a couple of references to Prudence from which one gleans that:

- Prudence was a Director of Heals
- She was in charge of the Mansard Gallery from its start in 1917
- She was still central to Heals' activities post-WWII when, with Tom Worthington she set up its Wholesale & Export subsidiary, which was to become internationally renowned as Heals Fabrics.

Has she been largely written out of the picture because she was Ambrose Heal's long term mistress OR, vice versa, was it that as his mistress she was given a number of sinecure posts that she did not quite merit? Whichever, [I favour the former], this appendix on 'her' Mansard Gallery is at least to register her as a possible 'show-off' personality, as well as providing a case study of how a London store used art and design to 'show-off' its wares.

There are examples of other stores attracting customers by putting on exhibitions or showing the work of famous artists in their windows; and a number, from time to time, would have craftsmen and women demonstrating how items of their merchandise were made. Liberty's became particularly known, after WWII, for its 'showing off' of contemporary European design,

Prudence Mauffe with Tom Worthington of Heals' Fabrics.

Poster for London Group Exhibition, illus. Edward McKnight
Kauffer, 1919.

Announcement card for 1918 exhibition of the London Group,
illus. Edward McKnight Kauffer.

Group X poster, illus. McKnight Kauffer.

which included the furniture of the likes of Alvar Aalto, Arne Jacobsen and Gio Ponti. But it was Heal's Mansard Gallery, established at the top of its recently completed new building in 1917, that was to become a magnet, a permanent feature through to the 1970s for contemporary art and design. It not only showed the work of Heal's own designers and craftsmen, including that of Ambrose, himself, and his son Christopher, but acted as an exhibition space to be let out for short-term exhibitions.

Susanna Gooden wrote of the Mansard:

Exhibitions were extremely varied and managed to work on many levels – being inspiring to designers and educational to the general public, without being condescending; fashionable yet approachable; revolutionary but with inevitable commercial undertones.

From the start the Gallery was a space in which Heal's mounted their own exhibitions, let it out to artists, designers or exhibition curators, or to art and design related societies. For letting, the terms seem to have been either a straight rental fee [the tenant carrying all the expenses and supplying attendants], or that Heals took the entrance money and did not charge a hire fee as long as the renter spent an agreed amount on publicity [as well as supplying catalogues and attendants]. Heal's would have profited from either alternative for even if there were to be some small loss financially the kudos for showing 'the great and good' would inevitably pay off one way or another.

In hindsight, it is not always easy to see whether some exhibitions originated from Heals or from outsiders, but records show attendances rising from two or three thousands for the early shows, to tens of thousands through the 1930s. This meant increasing 'footprints' for Heals, footprints mounting above the ground floor, an achievement that was always to be something of a challenge for London stores. Heals must have been particularly pleased when the Sitwell brothers, Osbert and Sacheverall staged their exhibition of French art in the Mansard Gallery in 1919, with some three hundred works by some thirty-nine

Christmas poster, illus. Claud Lovat Fraser.

artists, the list now reading as a roll-call of 20th century French greats – Matisse, Derain, Dufy, Soutine, Leger, Utrillo, along with 'adopted' French – Picasso, Modigliani, Friez and Zadkine. The brothers, along with Herbert Read, manned the desk [presumably clutching the entrance fees in their well-manicured hands]. The exhibition caused a furor in the press with the *Times'* critic describing the works as 'ghastly'; however, all this must have been great for trade.

There was a similar uproar with the mounting of the Group X exhibition in 1920. Groupo X was a mixed bag of artists, including the runt of the pre-war Vorticists. Altogether more genteel was the annual renting of the gallery by the London Group, albeit behind the scenes were the power battles surrounding Roger Fry. These exhibitions brought in the Bloomsbury crowd and their aficionados. Virginia Wolf recorded her excitement at her first meeting with Aldous Huxley in the Gallery.

The Gallery, over the years, also provided a showcase for some of the Slade students. Ambrose Heal was wont to visit the art school which was in Gower Street, just round the back of Heals. For him this brought a personal benefit for he actually married a Slade student. The Mansard also became known for showing architecture, possibly linked to Prudence Maufe being married to Edward Maufe, the architect for the Heal's extension in 1937. A typical architectural show was that of 1931 – 'Recent British Architecture' – which not only included work by Maufe but also by Giles Scott, Edwin Lutyens and Chermayeff.

The list of artists who showed, or were shown, at the Mansard Gallery is impressive, from a war-related print show in 1918 [which included Frank Brangwyn, C.R.W. Nevison and William Rothenstein] and a Claud Lovat Fraser one-man exhibition in 1919; through the '20s with the likes of Maxwell Armfield and Paul Nash; into the '30s with Rodrigo Moynihan and Epstein, along with Edward Bawden and Eric Ravilious, who showed their cartoons for Morley College murals; and into the post-war period when Mary Fedden, an ex-Slade student, was given her first exhibition there.

Claud Lovat Fraser poster for his solo exhibition in 1919.

Left
Exhibition poster, 'Winter comforts in the home', *c.*1935, illust. Norman Weaver.

And then there were Heal's own annual shows in the Gallery for their own merchandise, entitled 'Modern Tendencies'. The *Times* wrote of the 1930 one:

> … there has been arranged at the Mansard Gallery … an exhibition to illustrate 'Modern Tendencies in Furnishings'. As is usual at this establishment the Exhibition is very well arranged, one object being related to another as it would be in the house or flat and reproductions in colour after such artists as Gauguin and Van Gogh on the walls of the Gallery contribute to the atmosphere.

The Mansard Gallery was to sell prints throughout, and, in the early days, Frank Pick, of London Transport, a DIA friend of Ambrose Heal, would let him have surplus posters to sell there. In the inter-war years and the years immediately after WWII the Gallery was the 'happening' art space, and seems to have achieved its spin off function of getting customers to walk through the shop on the way to it if the words of Sir Lawrence Weaver, then President of DIA, were representative:

> Last summer I was taken there [Heals] by a friend to see a show in the Mansard Gallery and I strayed all over the floors …

He claimed never to have visited the store before.

Bibliography

A good deal of the material for this book comes from my own collection of journals – *Display*, *Store*, *Commercial Art*, *Art & Industry* and *Modern Publicity*. Here are other sources used:

1918 H. Gordon Selfridge, *The Romance of Commerce*.

1930 H. Stuart Menzies, *Let's Forget Business, the commentaries of Fortnum & Mason*, A&C Black Ltd.

1935 intro. Harry Trethowan, *Selling through the Window*, The Studio Ltd.

1938 Richard S. Lambert, *The Universal Provider*, George G. Harrap.

1942 Francis Marshall, *Fashion Drawing*, Studio Publications, How to do it series no. 30.

1952 Bryan & Norman Westwood, *The Modern Shop*, The Architectural Press.

1954 Natasha Kroll, *Window Display*, Studio Publications, How to do it series no. 51.

1956 Somaka & Hellberg, *Shops and Stores Today*, B.T. Batsford Ltd.

1960 D.W. Peel, *A Garden in the Sky, the story of Barkers of Kensington*, W.H. Allen

1960 Reginald Pound, *Selfridges, a biography*.

1964 Alison Adburgham, *Shops and Shopping*.

1975 ed. Alexandra Artley, *The Golden Age of Shop Design*, The Architectural Press.

1975 Alison Adburgham, *Liberty's, a biography of a shop*, George Allen & Unwin.

1975 Hermione Hobhouse, *A History of Regent Street*, Macdonald & Jane.

1978 Maurice Corina, *Fine Silks and Oak Counters: Debenhams, 1778–1978*, Hutchinson Benham.

1979 Alison Adburgham, *Shopping in Style*, Thames & Hudson.

1981 Tim Dale, *Harrods*, Harrods Publishing.

1983 Rosemary Ind, *Emberton*, Scolar Press.

1984 Gordon Honeycombe, *Selfridges: Seventy-five years*, Park Lane Press.

1984 Susanna Gooden, *At the Sign of the Four Poster, a history of Heals*, Heals & Son.

1989 Michael K. Moss & Alison Turton, *A legend of Retailing, House of Fraser*, Weidenfeld & Nicholson.

1990 Berry Ritchie, *A Touch of Class, the story of Austin Reed*, James & James.

1992 ed. Stephen Calloway, *The House of Liberty, masters of style and decoration*, Thames & Hudson.

1996 David Wainwright, *The British Tradition: Simpson – a world of style*, Quiller Press.

1996 J. Hewitt, *The Commercial Art of Tom Purvis*, Manchester Metropolitan University Press.

2001 Clair Masset, *Department Stores*.

2002 ed. Christoph Gruneberg and Max Hellein, *Shopping*, Hatje Cantz.

2005 Paul Jobling, *Man Appeal, advertising, modernism and menswear*, Berg.

2007 Lindy Woodhead, *Shopping, Seduction & Mr. Selfridge*, Profile Books.

2007 Peyton Skipworth, *Entertaining a la Carte, Edward Bawden and Fortnum & Mason*, The Mainstone Press.

2010 Judith Clark and Amy de la Haye, *Jaeger 125*.

Acknowledgements

My thanks are due to the generosity, time, interest and effort of:

Alison Kenney at the City of Westminster Archive Centre

Eve Watson at the Royal Society of Arts Archives

Sebastian Wormwell at the Harrods Archives

Anna Buruma at the Liberty's Archives

Catherine Moriarty and Lesley Whitworth at the Design Archives, University of Brighton

Katie Hudson at Harvey Nichols

Judy Faraday at the John Lewis Partnership Archives

Joanathan Carmichael at Jaeger's

The staff at the V&A Archive of Art & Design

… and countless well-informed friends including Brian Webb; Pat Schleger; my ever additive book designer, David Preston; and a number of chatty London taxi drivers who, as ever, had their opinions on the subject.

Opposite
Fougasse poster, 'Please shop early', London Transport, 1937.

Don't get your Whitsun shopping mixed up
with your Coronation rejoicing.
PLEASE SHOP EARLY ⊖